Getting Around

If you see a plus sign (+) between two keys, you muhe second key, and then release both keys. If you see a[...] first key, press and release the next key, and so on.

Press ...	To move ...
↑	Up one line
↓	Down one line
→	Right a character
←	Left one character
Ctrl+→	To the beginning of the next word
Ctrl+←	To the beginning of the previous word
Home	To the beginning of the line
End	To the end of the line

Press ...	To move ...
Ctrl+↑	Up one paragraph
Ctrl+↓	Down one paragraph
Page Up	Up one screenful of text
Page Down	Down one screenful of text
Alt+Page Up	Up one page
Alt+Page Down	Down one page
Ctrl+Home	To the top of the document
Ctrl+End	To the end of the document

Deleting Text Shortcuts

If you have selected text, you don't have to press Delete or Backspace to get rid of it. Just begin typing new text to replace it. Use these shortcuts to get rid of text you haven't selected.

Press ...	To delete ...
Backspace	Character to the left
Delete	Character to the right
Ctrl+Backspace	Current word

Press ...	To delete ...
Ctrl+Delete	From insertion point to the end of a line
Ctrl+Shift+Delete	From insertion point to the end of a page

Selecting Text Tricks

If you want to delete or change existing text, you'll usually need to select it first. You can hold down the Shift key while using the regular insertion point-movement keys to select text, or you can use these tricks:

If you want to ...	Do this ...
Select a word	Double-click the word.
Select a sentence	Triple-click the sentence.
Select a paragraph	Click four times on the paragraph.

If you want to ...	Do this ...
Select a line	Move the pointer to the left of the line and click.
Select a page	Choose Edit, Select, Page.
Select everything	Choose Edit, Select, All.

Common Formatting Tasks

If you want to ...	Do this ...
Make text bold	Press Ctrl+B, type the text, and press Ctrl+B. Or select the existing text, and then press Ctrl+B.
Underline text	Press Ctrl+U, type the text, and press Ctrl+U. Or select the existing text, and then press Ctrl+U.
Make text italic	Press Ctrl+I, type the text, and press Ctrl+I. Or select the existing text, and then press Ctrl+I.
Indent a paragraph	Press F7 to indent on left side only. Press Ctrl+Shift+F7 to indent on left and right sides.
Center a line	Choose Layout, Line, Center, and type the text.
Right-justify text	Choose Layout, Line, Flush Right, and type the text.
Add page numbering	Choose Layout, Page, Numbering. Click and hold on the wide button by Position; then choose a page number location that suits you. Choose OK.

If you want to ...	Do this ...
Change margins	Choose Layout, Margins. Type the margins you want to change in inches, then choose OK.
Change line spacing	Choose Layout, Line, Spacing. Type the spacing you want (1 for single spacing, 2 for double spacing, and so on). Choose OK.
Center a page	Choose Layout, Page, Center. Click on the Current Page radio button, and then choose OK.
Use a different font	Choose Layout, Font. Scroll through the Font Face list and select the font you want. Click a size you want in the Font Size list. When the sample box in the lower left corner of the dialog box shows text in the size and look you want, choose OK.

Common Editing Tasks

If you want to ...	Do this ...
Insert a code so that the date is always current	Choose Insert, Date, Date Code.
Insert date text that stays the same	Choose Insert, Date, Date Text.
Start a new page	Press Ctrl+Enter.
Check your spelling	Choose Tools, Speller, Start.

If you want to ...	Do this ...
Find a word	Choose Edit, Find, type the word, and choose Find Next.
Replace all occurrences of one word/phrase with another	Choose Edit, Replace, type the text to be replaced, press Tab; type the replacement text; choose Replace All.

Dawn Steinke

I HATE

WORDPERFECT® FOR WINDOWS™

Elden Nelson

I Hate WordPerfect for Windows

Copyright ©1993 by Que® Corporation

Library of Congress Catalog No.: 93-86076

ISBN: 1-56529-391-6

95 94 93   6 5 4 3 2 1

Interpretation of the printing code: the rightmost double-digit number is the year of the book's printing; the rightmost single-digit number, the number of the book's printing. For example, a printing code of 93-1 shows that the first printing of the book occurred in 1993.

Screen reproductions in this book were created by using Collage Plus from Inner Media, Inc., Hollis, NH.

This book is based on WordPerfect Corporation's WordPerfect 5.2 for Windows.

Publisher: David P. Ewing

Associate Publisher: Rick Ranucci

Director of Publishing: Mike Miller

Managing Editor: Corinne Walls

Marketing Manager: Ray Robinson

Dedication

To my son or daughter—whichever you turn out to be (just one more month 'til we find out). Welcome.

I HATE WORDPERFECT FOR WINDOWS!

Credits

Publishing Manager
Shelley O'Hara

Acquisitions Editor
Thomas F. Godfrey III

Production Editor
Cindy Morrow

Copy Editors
Elsa M. Bell
Tom Hayes
Patrick Kanouse
Joy Preacher
Linda Seifert

Technical Editor
Linda Hefferin

Book Designer
Amy Peppler-Adams

Cover Designer
Tim Amrhein

Cover Illustration
Jeff MacNelly

Production Team
Angela Bannan
Danielle Bird
Paula Carroll
Laurie Casey
Charlotte Clapp
Teresa Forrester
Michelle Greenwalt
Heather Kaufman
Bob LaRoche
Tim Montgomery
Caroline Roop
Dennis Sheehan
Amy L. Steed
Tina Trettin
Sue VandeWalle
Mary Beth Wakefield
Lillian Yates

Indexer
Michael Hughes

Novice Reviewer
P.J. Marchesseault

Editorial Assistant
Julia Blount

Composed in *Goudy* and *MCPdigital* by Que Corporation.

About the Author

Elden Nelson is just a regular guy who has somehow stumbled into the strange profession of knowing a lot about computers, and especially WordPerfect. He's written a couple macro manuals for WordPerfect Corporation, writes a monthly column for *WordPerfect for Windows Magazine*, and has worked with WordPerfect's famed Customer Support team, where he learned to sympathize with the struggles of WordPerfect users and solve their problems.

Elden drives a red Mazda Miata, plays a reasonable game of raquetball, is a master of the barbecue grill, is 5'8" tall, has brown hair and eyes, speaks fluent Finnish, and has never been convicted of a felony. Any questions?

Acknowledgements

Thanks to everyone in the Que staff who not only does a fantastic job of turning my garbled manuscript into nice-looking books, but also puts up with me on a day-to-day basis. Special thanks go to Shelley O'Hara and Cindy Morrow, who had a direct hand in massaging this book into what you are currently holding in your hot little hands.

Dell Computers loaned me a second computer while I wrote this book, so that I could look at what's happening in WordPerfect on one computer screen and write on another. (Sure, it makes my office look like the NASA control center, but it makes writing much easier.) In fact, the computer they loaned me is much nicer than the one I own. So now I've got a severe case of computer envy. Thanks especially to Denise McLaughlin at Dell for getting the computer to me so quickly and on such short notice.

Thanks to Lisa Bearnson of *WordPerfect Magazine* and Allen Biehl of *WordPerfect for Windows Magazine* for letting deadlines slip while I wrote this book. I owe what remains of my sanity to you.

And, thanks especially to Susan, my spouse, for being patient, even-tempered, easy-to-be-with, and generally magnificent, even while being several months pregnant.

Trademark Acknowledgments

All terms mentioned in this book that are known to be trademarks or service marks have been appropriately capitalized. Que cannot attest to the accuracy of this information. Use of a term in this book should not be regarded as affecting the validity of any trademark or service mark.

MS-DOS and Microsoft Windows are registered trademarks of Microsoft Corporation.

IBM and IBM PC are registered trademarks of International Business Machines Corporation.

WordPerfect is a registered trademark of WordPerfect Corporation.

Contents at a Glance

Table of Contents

Introduction

"Oh no! Not again!"

"This computer won't do what I want!"

"Aaargh!"

"I hate WordPerfect for Windows!"

Sound familiar? Welcome to the club. Computers are confusing. WordPerfect for Windows is confusing. But they don't have to be. If you hate WordPerfect for Windows, you'll love this book. This is a book for people who don't want to read about WordPerfect for Windows. After all, you don't want to devote your life to your computer—you just want to type a letter.

The idea behind this book is that there's way too much in WordPerfect for Windows for any sane person to learn. This book has weeded out the bizarre, esoteric stuff and left you with the absolute essentials: bite-sized chunks of WordPerfect wisdom you can use to get your work done now. And as an extra bonus, it's actually fun to read, so you won't instantly fall asleep every time you flip the thing open.

What about Those Drawings in the Margin?

All the information in this book is not created equal. Occasionally, the book includes something more technical than the other stuff. This book uses *icons* (those are the funny drawings within the margins) to say things like, "Hey, this is technical stuff. You don't have to read it." The book has other icons that tell you when to be careful, alert you to some frustrating WordPerfect function that you'll have to deal with, and so on.

Here are the pictures and what they mean:

This little puppy pops up whenever the book has to explain something frustrating or confusing about WordPerfect. It's a good idea to read the text next to this icon; it'll help you brace yourself for things to come.

You'll see this icon next to extra-helpful tips—things you can use to make your life easier.

CAUTION

"Beware! Warning! Danger, Will Robinson!" is this icon's message. It can help you avoid WordPerfect pitfalls and potholes.

EXPERTS ONLY

If you're in the mood to read more detailed information on something about WordPerfect for Windows, seek out the material flagged with this icon. This is interesting, useful stuff, but it's more advanced, and you don't have to know this information in order to use WordPerfect well.

BUZZWORDS

BUZZWORD

Computer people have made up hundreds of new words, as well as given strange new meanings to a lot of old words. This picture alerts you that one of these mysterious new terms is about to be explained.

PART I

A Crash Course in WordPerfect for Windows

Includes:

1: Things You *Must* Know to Use WordPerfect

2: Editing Essentials

3: Formatting Fundamentals

4: Printing

5: Help Me!

CHAPTER 1

Things You Must Know to Use WordPerfect

IN A NUTSHELL

▼ Start Windows
▼ Get WordPerfect for Windows up and running
▼ Use the mouse
▼ Learn to use menus and dialog boxes
▼ Practice typing text
▼ Save your work
▼ Quit WordPerfect for Windows

So, you hate WordPerfect for Windows. Maybe you've tried to use WordPerfect for Windows a few times and feel frustrated at your inability to make it do what you want. Or maybe you've never even tried to use it; you just know you'll hate it and have managed to spare yourself the agony. (I myself have never tasted Brussels sprouts for this very reason.)

In either case, you've somehow gotten yourself into a predicament: you have to use WordPerfect for Windows. What do you do now? Stop worrying. You've already made the right first move—you bought this book. (Or, if you haven't, why haven't you? Stop browsing and buy it!)

This chapter starts at the very beginning and guides you through the basics of WordPerfect for Windows. You learn how to start Windows and WordPerfect for Windows, understand the things you see on your screen, and write in WordPerfect for Windows. You also learn how to save your work and get out of the program. Once you can do all these things, you're half way to being computer literate.

Starting Windows

Before you can start WordPerfect for Windows, you need to have your computer running Windows.

BUZZWORDS

WINDOWS

Windows is the name of a program Microsoft created to make Bill Gates, the owner of Microsoft, rich. This scheme worked—just about everybody uses it, and Bill Gates is indeed rich. Why is this program called "Windows?" Because every type of information your computer displays is in some

kind of box; these boxes look like windows to mentally deranged computer programmers who should probably spend more time outdoors.

When you run Windows, your computer becomes easier to use—instead of typing bizarre commands, you use a mouse to click on pictures.

How you start Windows depends on what your computer screen looks like when you turn on the computer. Here are some ways your computer might appear.

Ways to start Windows

✔ **If you get a dark screen with a C:\> and a blinking bar,** you're in DOS—the computer equivalent of hell. To start Windows, just type **WIN** and press Enter.

✔ **If a menu or list of options appears,** look to see whether one of those options is Windows. If so, press the letter or number by that option. You may also need to press Enter afterward.

✔ **If something like the following picture appears,** you must have been born under a lucky star—your computer *automatically* starts Windows. You don't have to do anything to start it. More and more computers come this way.

I HATE WORDPERFECT FOR WINDOWS!

The Program
Manager

Double-click here
to start
WordPerfect
for Windows

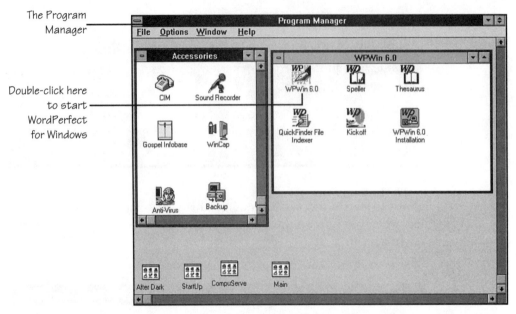

"I HATE THIS!"

That's not what my screen looks like!

Your screen might look different than the preceding picture—
no problem. The important thing is that the screen shows a
box with *Program Manager* at the top and an icon (small
picture) with *WPWin 6.0* inside.

Mousing Around

If you're going to work with Windows—as well as WordPerfect for
Windows—you've got to learn to be comfortable with using a mouse.

The mouse is no big deal to master. Just think of it as the computer equivalent of your hand. As you roll the mouse on the table, a mouse pointer moves around on the screen.

"I HATE THIS!"

My mouse is dead!

If you have a mouse but nothing happens on-screen when you move it, your copy of Windows isn't set up properly to use a mouse. Trying to set up your machine yourself can be a royal pain. I recommend that you do whatever is necessary (whine, wheedle, beg, bribe) to get a technically oriented person to handle the setup.

Basic mouse maneuvers

✔ **Point:** Roll your mouse on your desk so that the on-screen pointer is positioned over an on-screen object. You almost always follow pointing the mouse with something else—like clicking or dragging.

✔ **Click:** Press the left mouse button once. You click on something to "choose" it. The chosen item often appears highlighted.

✔ **Drag:** When a man dresses as a woman. No, wait, that's the wrong *drag*. To drag, move the mouse pointer to a beginning point, press and hold down the left mouse button, and then move the mouse pointer to a different place. This whole procedure is often called *click and drag*. You use this technique to highlight text in WordPerfect for Windows.

✔ **Double-click**: Press the left mouse button twice in a row, very quickly. Double-clicking is used for a whole slew of stuff: to launch programs, to select a word, and to choose options in lists, just to name a few.

Starting WordPerfect for Windows (Click click here)

Starting WordPerfect for Windows isn't too difficult. Once you've got Windows started, find the WPWin 6.0 icon. (Remember that "icon" is just fancy computer talk for "small drawing.") The icon (which is sitting by other icons in the same box) looks like this:

WPWin 6.0

"I HATE THIS!"

I don't see that icon!

If you can't find the icon, it's probably hiding. Here's how to make it appear: First, press Alt+W. A list (called a *menu*) appears at the top of your screen. One of the options in this list is **WPWin 6.0**. Next, on your keyboard, press the number to the left of this option. A window appears, and one of the items in that window is the WPWin 6.0 icon.

Now, take your mouse in hand, move the mouse pointer over to the WPWin 6.0 icon, and click the left mouse button twice in a row—very quickly. This is called *double-clicking*. If nothing happens, try again, but this time be sure to keep the mouse very still, and make the clicks a little closer together.

Looking Around (What's all this junk on my screen?)

When you first start WordPerfect for Windows, your computer clicks and grinds and shimmies for a minute. Then some funky stuff appears at the top of the screen; the rest of the screen is practically blank. Not very exciting.

When you get to know the program, however, you'll be pleasantly surprised at how useful WordPerfect for Windows is. Let's begin with a look at what's on-screen:

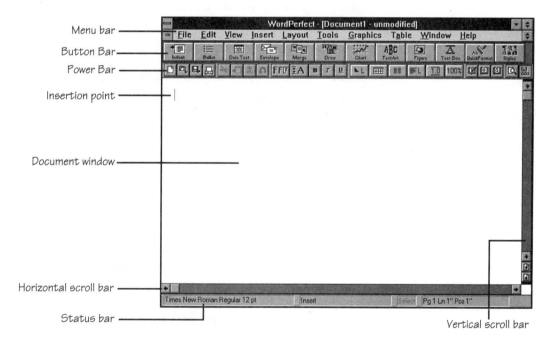

Menu bar
Button Bar
Power Bar
Insertion point
Document window
Horizontal scroll bar
Status bar
Vertical scroll bar

✔ The **menu bar** is the way you'll get to most of WordPerfect's features. Just move the mouse pointer to a word in the menu bar and click the left mouse button. A list of commands pops on the screen. Then just click on the command you want to use.

✔ The **Button Bar** is designed to make your life easier. Each of the buttons on the Button Bar represents a WordPerfect for Windows feature. When you click on a button, WordPerfect for Windows starts the feature right away—no wading through menus. Using the Button Bar is usually a lot faster and easier than remembering which menu contains a certain command. And if that's not enough, when you move the mouse pointer over a button—without clicking on the button—the top of the screen gives you a brief description of what the button does.

✔ The **Power Bar**—which sounds like something you might eat before heading to the gym to work out—is a row of buttons that provides quick access to most WordPerfect for Windows features. Instead of just having buttons, like the Button Bar, the Power Bar also has drop-down menus for fonts and making tables and whatnot. (This book points out whenever you can use the Power Bar to accomplish something more quickly.)

✔ The **document window** is where you actually do your typing. Not very big, is it? Does this mean you're going to be forever restricted to typing two-paragraph memos? Nope. As you begin typing, your text moves down the screen until you fill up the document window. Then, the stuff at the top of the window moves up and out of sight—as if it were being rolled up on a giant scroll. Don't worry, though, it's still there, and you can get back to it when you need it.

✔ Think of the **insertion point** as an on-screen "You Are Here" arrow. The insertion point moves as you type, left to right, one space at a time. It tells you where the next letter you type will appear.

✔ The **scroll bars** let you easily move around in your document. The vertical scroll bar helps you move up and down through the document; the horizontal bar helps you move from side to side. Chapter 2 gives you the dirt on using the scroll bars.

✔ The **status bar** provides all kinds of pieces of information—the most important being how much you've typed. On the right side of the status bar, you see something that looks like this:

```
Pg 1 Ln 1" Pos 1"
```

These letters and numbers tell you where your insertion point is located. `Pg` might *seem* to be the rating of your document (as in `Pg-13`); it's really just what page you're on. `Ln` means "Line." This number tells you how many inches you are from the top of the page. Because WordPerfect for Windows automatically sets up one-inch margins all the way around your document, this area shows `1"` when you're at the top of a page. `Pos` means "Position." This number tells you how many inches you are from the left side of the page.

Ordering from the Menu

You're going to spend most of your time in this program just typing. Easy enough. But sometimes you'll want to do something different, like change margins or set up new tab stops. When you need to do more than type, use the menu bar at the top of the screen. The menu bar looks like this:

| File Edit View Insert Layout Tools Graphics Table Window Help |

With a mouse, choosing menus is a cinch. Just point at one of the words in the menu bar, and then click. This is called "choosing" the menu. For example, if you want to choose the Help menu, you just click on the word Help in the menu bar, and the menu drops down, like this:

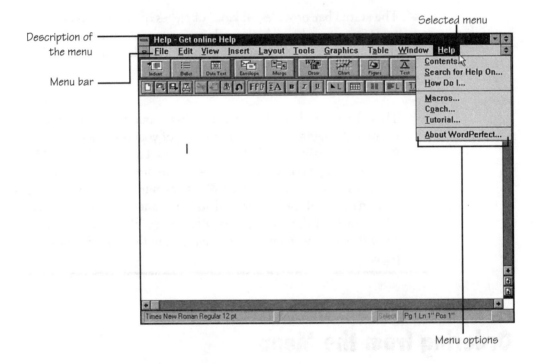

You then choose—by clicking—the menu option you want. For example, if you want a WordPerfect for Windows tutorial, you choose Tutorial.

✔ If you want to keep your hands at the keyboard, you can choose a menu by pressing an Alt+*letter* key combo. You just have to find which letter in the menu is underlined. For example, since the H in **H**elp is underlined, you press Alt+H. (To press the Alt+H key combination, press and hold down the Alt key, press H, and then release both keys.) You can then choose one of the options from the menu by pressing the underlined letter; you don't have to hold down Alt when you choose the menu option.

✔ In the rest of this book, I word menu selections like this: Choose **H**elp, **T**utorial. When you see a sentence like this, click **H**elp in the menu bar, and then click **T**utorial in the Help menu.

✔ If you pull down a menu and then decide you don't want it after all, you can make the menu disappear by pressing the Alt key by itself.

✔ Some words in menus end in a series of three dots (...). When you choose these options, something called a *dialog box* pops up on-screen. You learn about dialog boxes in the next section in this chapter.

✔ Some menu options have a triangle to the right of the option name; if you choose one of these options, a menu pops out to the right of the option. You can choose one of the options from this new menu in the same way you would from a regular menu.

Dealing with Dialog Boxes

Often, when you choose an option in a menu, a *dialog box* appears. Here's an example of how a dialog box looks:

Buttons

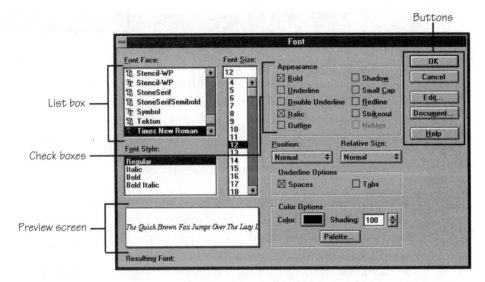

List box

Check boxes

Preview screen

Each dialog box has buttons; many have check boxes and places to type; and some have other strange bells and whistles. By doing various kinds of things in these boxes, you're turning on—and off—various WordPerfect for Windows features. You use different parts of dialog boxes in different ways, and it helps to know the tricks behind using them.

HUH?

BUZZWORDS

DEFAULT

The option that is chosen automatically in WordPerfect unless you choose something different. In most dialog boxes, the OK button is the default. You can just press Enter to choose this button. If you want to select a different button, you have to make an effort to choose it.

Those wacky dialog box options

✔ **Command buttons.** Buttons that you "press" to make something happen. Every dialog box has at least one button. You press a command button by using the mouse to click on it, or by pressing Alt plus the underlined letter on the button. In this book, I tell you to "choose" the button you need to press. OK and Cancel are common command buttons.

✔ **Check boxes.** Little boxes that you select if you want to turn on a feature. You check a box by using the mouse to click on it. You can also check it by pressing Alt plus the underlined letter in the text describing the check box. You use these same procedures to uncheck a box (and turn off the feature).

✔ **Radio buttons.** Buttons that let you choose a mutually exclusive feature. If you choose one radio button, all the others in that group are automatically turned off, like when you punch buttons on a radio. In the same way you can only listen to one radio station at a time, you can only choose one radio button from a group. To choose a radio button, use the mouse to click in the circle beside the text that describes the feature. Or, if you're a keyboard-type person, press Alt plus the underlined letter in the button name.

✔ **Pop-up menus.** Menus of additional available choices. You make the menu pop up by clicking the menu's down-arrow button, or—if you prefer the keyboard—pressing the underlined letter beside the menu. When the menu appears, double-click on the option you want; or use your arrow keys to highlight the option, and then press Enter.

✔ **List boxes.** Large boxes that contain several choices. When you need to choose one of those options, click on the option. If the option is the last choice you are making in the dialog box, double-click on the option.

continues

19

I HATE WORDPERFECT FOR WINDOWS!

Those wacky dialog box options (continued)

✔ **Text boxes.** Boxes in which you type a word or number. To begin typing in a text box, click the mouse where the text needs to go or press the underlined letter shown in the text beside where the text goes. Then just type away.

TIP

Pop-up menus and list boxes usually contain more items than can be displayed at once. If more items are available, a scroll bar appears on the right side of the list. You can see more of the list by clicking on the up and down arrow buttons.

"I HATE THIS!"

Some options look dim!

Certain parts of a dialog box may be light gray—as if one of the light bulbs in the dialog box burned out. Don't panic. Nothing is wrong with WordPerfect for Windows. The program is just telling you that the feature is currently inappropriate right now, and therefore isn't available. For example, if you've got the Print dialog box up, the Selected Text radio button will be gray—and therefore unavailable—when you don't have text selected.

Typing Text (Writing the Great American Novel)

Typing in WordPerfect for Windows is much like using your type-writer—but easier. First, you don't press Enter (on some old keyboards, Enter is called *Return*) at the end of each line. WordPerfect for Windows automatically "wraps" the text to the next line. To see how WordPerfect

for Windows knows when to go to the next line, type frantically at the keyboard for a minute. Try typing the following text without pressing Enter:

> **Judy, listening intently to the company president give the yearly review, realized she preferred Cocoa Puffs to Count Chocula.**

As you type, the insertion point moves to the right, outrunning the letters. As you get to the end of a line, WordPerfect for Windows knows the line should end and zips down to the beginning of the next line. (The place where a line ends is called a *soft return*, but who cares?) Later, when you add text or make changes to the text, WordPerfect for Windows adjusts the line breaks.

You add text simply by typing it. As you type, everything in front of the insertion point (the text you typed previously) is pushed down to clear space for the new text. This is perhaps the second most wonderful thing about using a word processor—and it's environmentally correct! Think of all the paper (and therefore trees) it saves—no more crumpled paper filling the garbage can! Oh yeah. If you're wondering what the first most wonderful thing about a word processor is, it's that you can make your mouse pointer dance around on the screen when you're bored or have writer's block. Now that's entertainment!

Don't completely forget about the Enter key. You still need it in certain situations—to separate paragraphs, for example. Simply press the Enter key when you want a paragraph to end.

You also use the Enter key to add blank lines between lines of text—and to end lines before they wrap to the next line. For example, a name or address usually doesn't go from margin to margin. Instead, you type your name and press Enter. The insertion point moves to the beginning of the next line, where you type your address.

BUZZWORDS

HARD RETURNS

When you want to end a paragraph, you press Enter. The end of the paragraph is called a *hard return*, although there's nothing hard about it. A hard return is different from the kind of returns that WordPerfect for Windows inserts automatically at the end of lines—these are called *soft returns*. If you insert or delete text, soft returns are adjusted; hard returns aren't.

Save Your Work, Save Your Sanity

If anything can make you hate WordPerfect for Windows (as well as computers in general), losing your hard work is it. Imagine that you've been working on a report. You're typing along faster than you ever have before—after all, you need to be finished in 57 minutes. Suddenly, lightening strikes and knocks out the power in your office. What happens to all your hard work?

The fact is, every time the computer is turned off—whether on purpose or by accident—it forgets everything. If there's a power failure or your computer unexpectedly "locks up" (refuses to budge because of some problem with the program), you could very well lose all your typing. You can't keep lightning from striking, so to prevent the loss of hours of work, you need to save your document often.

Save means to take the document you've been typing and store a copy of it on your hard disk. You never see your hard disk because it's permanently bolted into the insides of your computer—just think of it as a big filing cabinet inside your computer.

After you save a document, you can retrieve it and come back to your work another time.

BUZZWORDS

DOCUMENT

Unless you are in the legal field, you probably aren't used to referring to pieces of writing as *documents*. You probably wouldn't say "Jane, get me the Company Picnic Document." In computerese, a *document* is any piece of writing—a poem, memo, letter, report. A document can be of any length—one line, a couple paragraphs, several pages.

Saving a Document

This is how you save a document:

1. Choose **File**, **Save**; or click the Save button in the Power Bar.

The Save As dialog box appears with some letters highlighted in the Filename text box. This is WordPerfect's suggestion of what you should name the document—a silly suggestion.

2. Type a file name, such as **MYFIRST**.

As soon as you begin typing, the old highlighted text disappears. Type a word that reminds you of what the document is about. You must follow some strict rules when naming files. You can use up to an eight-character name; you can't use spaces; and you shouldn't use punctuation. (If you're confused on this naming-files thing, flip to Chapter 9 for the finer points of naming files.)

WordPerfect for Windows will assign an extension (last name) for your file of WPD. Don't change this extension. When you list your files later, WordPerfect for Windows shows only the files with the WPD extension.

BUZZWORDS

EXTENSION

When you name your documents, you can use eight letters, a period, and then another three letters. The period and last three letters is called an "extension." WordPerfect for Windows automatically gives your documents an extension of WPD, so you don't have to bother typing one.

3. Choose OK or press Enter.

After you save your document, your work appears on-screen again. Meanwhile, the name you gave it (and some information about where it's kept) appears at the top of the screen—right by the name of the program.

Saving Suggestions

Here are some suggestions on how, when, and why to save:

Checklist

✔ After you've saved a document once, you need to keep updating it. Save your work every 10 minutes or three paragraphs. To update your documents, just choose **File, Save**; or click the Save button on the Power Bar.

✔ As an extra-bonus way of saving/updating your documents, press Ctrl+S. If you're saving the document for the first time, the Save As dialog box appears; enter a name for the file into this dialog box. If you've already given the document a name, pressing Ctrl+S updates your work without further fuss.

✔ It's important to make your document names memorable. After a while, you'll have a lot of documents—each with a different name—and you can easily confuse and forget names. You might want to name a document FRED, for example, if you're writing a letter to your Uncle Fred.

✔ You can type the name in uppercase or lowercase. When the file name is displayed on-screen and in file lists, it appears in all upper-case no matter how you type it.

✔ If you type a name that's already been used, a box appears that asks whether you want to replace the file name; you can choose either Yes and No. If you want to replace the file you've saved previously with the file on-screen, choose Yes. If you don't or you are not sure, choose No; then type in a different name.

✔ You can learn the gory details of saving and files in Chapter 9, "Working with Files."

Exiting Documents and WordPerfect for Windows (Get me outta here!)

You can work on one letter for only so long. Then your sentences begin to read, "See Spot. See Spot run. See Spot run some more."

It's definitely time to work on something else, or better yet, to take a break and go catch up with the Flintstones.

Here's how to leave your document and WordPerfect for Windows:

1. Choose **File, Exit.**

2. If you've made changes to your document since you last saved your work, a box appears asking if you want to save changes. Choose **Yes** so that the next time you work on this document, it will be up to date.

TIP

If you just want to leave *this* document and work on a different one instead, choose **File, Close.** WordPerfect for Windows remains on-screen. You can start typing in a new, blank document.

TIP

When you leave WordPerfect for Windows, you might want to leave Windows as well. Here's how: at the Program Manager, choose **File, Exit.** A dialog box comes up, warning, "This will end your Windows session." Choose OK to tell the computer that you're glad you're ending the Windows session. Your computer will go dark, then you're back at the menacing DOS prompt. Now you can turn off your computer.

EXPERTS ONLY

Lots of Documents

You can have more than one document open at a time in WordPerfect for Windows. When you want to leave WordPerfect for Windows, the dialog box with the "Save Changes?" question appears for each document you have open. Choose Yes for each of them so that all your documents will be updated.

CHAPTER 2

Editing Essentials
(Rewriting History)

IN A NUTSHELL

▼ Open documents you've saved
▼ Move the insertion point
▼ Select text
▼ Delete text
▼ Restore deleted text
▼ Move text to new places (cut, copy, and paste)

WordPerfect is an editor's dream. With it, you can start on a project one day and finish it another. You can move text from one place to another immediately—no scissors, paper, or glue required. You can slash words, lines, or even pages with the greatest of ease. And if you change your mind, you can reverse the situation faster than you can say, "Oops!"

This chapter shows you how to edit your text, turning your rough drafts into finely crafted prose that would make Shakespeare weep with joy.

Opening Your Documents

If you go through the trouble of writing a document and saving it to disk, chances are you figure that you'll need it again sometime. (Chapter 1 explains how to name and save your documents so that you can work on them later.) If you've saved lots of documents, however, it might be hard to find the one you want. To help you find the right document, WordPerfect lets you display a list of documents, and then choose one from that list. Here's how it's done:

1. Choose **File**, **Open**. Or, if you like using the Power Bar, click the Open button.

The File Open dialog box appears in the middle of the screen, with a list of documents you can choose from.

TIP

If you like to keep your hands on the keyboard, you can bring up the Open File dialog box by pressing Ctrl+O.

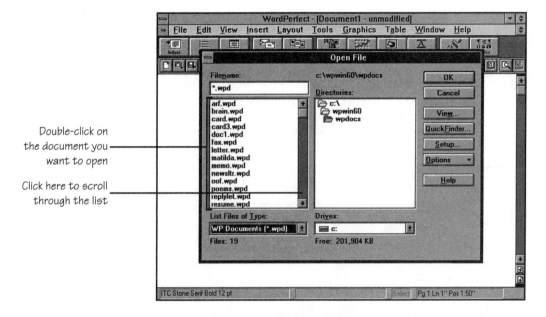

Double-click on the document you want to open

Click here to scroll through the list

2. Double-click the document you want.

If you haven't yet got the hang of double-clicking, you can click once on the file you want, and then choose the OK button.

Tips for opening documents

✔ The Filename list box can only show a few documents at a time. If you don't see the document you want, click on the up or down arrows at the right side of the list to see more of the list.

✔ If you want to open a document you've used very recently, just choose the File menu. The bottom of this menu shows the four documents you've most recently used. Choose the one you want.

continues

31

Tips for opening documents (continued)

✔ Usually, your documents are saved in one place on your hard disk, so everything's kept all nice and tidy. If you feel like a renegade, you can start creating directories and subdirectories to hold different kinds of documents. Chapter 9 shows you how to work through the directory maze.

TIP

The File Open dialog box is immensely powerful and useful—if you take the time to use it. You can move, copy, print, delete, and much, much more from here. If you're interested, Chapter 9 explains how to use this magnificent dialog box.

Cruising around the Document

One of the nice things about WordPerfect is how easily it lets you correct your mistakes. If you make a typo, you just move the insertion point back to where the problem is, erase it, and type the correct text. If you forget a word, move the insertion point to where the word should go and start typing; the text after the insertion point automatically gets pushed forward.

To do any editing, though, you need to move the insertion point to where you want the change. There are two good ways to move your insertion point. If you use a mouse, just click the pointer where you want to place the insertion point. When you only want to move the insertion point a little—a word or letter or two—using the arrow keys is faster and easier than using the mouse.

Look on your keyboard. You'll spot a cluster of arrow keys pointing in different directions (up, down, left, and right). These keys show up in different places on different keyboards, in accordance with the computer manufacturer mandate that no two keyboards look or work exactly the same. On most keyboards, the arrow keys are in their own lonely little cluster just to the right of the letter keys.

Basically, the insertion point moves in the direction indicated by the arrow:

Key	The Insertion Point Moves...
→	One letter to the right
←	One letter to the left
↓	One line down
↑	One line up

Moving, moving, moving

✔ You can't move the insertion point past the end of the last word in the document. The insertion point only goes as far as you've typed.

✔ If you hold down an arrow key, it goes completely berserk. For example, if you hold down the up-arrow key, the insertion point begins rocketing toward the top of the document. The insertion point continues its mad ascent until you release the key.

continues

✔ If you press the left-arrow key when you're already at the left edge of the page, the insertion point moves to the right edge of the page, one line up.

✔ If you have more than a screenful of text and you press the right-arrow key when the insertion point is at the right edge of a line, the insertion point goes to the left side of the page, one line down.

✔ If the insertion point is at the top of the screen and you press the up-arrow key, the text moves down (computer types call this *scrolling*) so that you can see the text above it. Pressing the down-arrow key when you're at the bottom of the document produces the opposite effect: the old text moves up so that you can see the text below it.

Using Speed Movement Keys

When you start writing your Great American Novel (or at least creating long documents), you'll find that using the arrow keys to move your insertion point through large sections of text is too-o-o slo-o-o-ow. WordPerfect has several difficult-to-remember keystroke combinations that quickly get you from one place to another. Although these keystrokes initially seem complicated, after some practice, your fingers will remember them.

Key or key combo	What the key or combo does
Ctrl+Home	Moves the insertion point to the top of your document.
Ctrl+End	Moves the insertion point to the end of your document.
Ctrl+→	Moves the insertion point to the beginning of the next word.
Ctrl+←	Moves the insertion point to the beginning of the previous word. In case you were wondering, there are no key combinations to move to the end of the next or previous word.
Ctrl+↑	Moves the insertion point to the beginning of the previous paragraph.
Ctrl+↓	Moves the insertion point to the beginning of the next paragraph.
Page Down	Moves the insertion point down a screenful of text. This is handy when you're finished reading all the text on-screen and you want to read the next screenful of text.
Page Up	Moves the insertion point up a screenful of text.

Scrollin', Scrollin', Scrollin'

The keyboard is okay, but most people's favorite way of moving around in the document is to use the vertical scroll bar. With it, you can move through the document at incredible rates, and with pretty good precision.

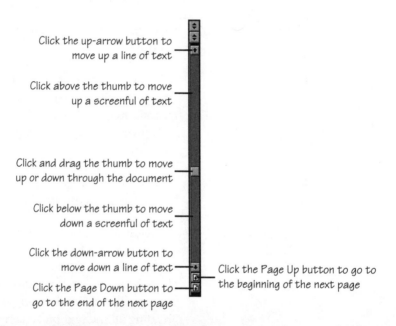

Click the up-arrow button to move up a line of text

Click above the thumb to move up a screenful of text

Click and drag the thumb to move up or down through the document

Click below the thumb to move down a screenful of text

Click the down-arrow button to move down a line of text

Click the Page Down button to go to the end of the next page

Click the Page Up button to go to the beginning of the next page

Scribblings on scrolling

✔ Scrolling is best for when you need to move your insertion point a considerable distance in your document. If you need to move just a paragraph or two, you're better off using the insertion point keys or just clicking in the right place with the mouse.

✔ Using the scroll bar just *locates* the place you're looking for; it doesn't automatically put your insertion point there. Once you've found the place you want, be sure to click there with your mouse pointer. If you don't, when you start typing you'll find the insertion point back where it was before you started scrolling.

✔ The scroll bar "thumb"—the square box in the scroll bar—is good for moving a general distance up or down the document. For example, if you want to move about half way through your document, click on the thumb and drag it to the halfway point of the scroll bar. If you want to go to the beginning of a document, drag the thumb to the top of the scroll bar; if you want to go all the way to the end of a document, drag the thumb to the bottom of the document.

✔ Clicking anywhere in the scroll bar *above* the thumb makes WordPerfect show the screenful of text above what you're currently looking at. Clicking in the scroll bar *below* the thumb moves you down a screenful.

✔ If you click and hold the mouse button in the scroll bar or in the up- and down-arrow buttons, the action begins to repeat very quickly. If you click and hold with your pointer on the up-arrow button, for example, WordPerfect scrolls up very quickly, one line at a time.

✔ The horizontal scroll bar works the same way as the vertical scroll bar, but you'll hardly ever need to use it. Usually you can see the left and right side of the text without scrolling.

Correcting Small Mistakes
(Throw your White-Out in the trash)

I'm a lousy typist. I tend to hit the "C" when I mean to type "V," and it's pretty much a coin toss as to whether I land on the right key when I aim for the "M."

It's okay to be a miserable typist in WordPerfect. Cleaning up typos and removing an unwanted word are easy. You just have to become handy with the Backspace and Delete keys.

Pressing the Backspace key removes the character to the *left* of the insertion point. The Backspace key is located in the upper right corner of the letters part of your keyboard. Some Backspace keys are kind enough to be labeled with the word *Backspace*, while others have nothing but an arrow pointing left. Do not confuse this key with the left-arrow key, which does not delete text.

Pressing Delete removes the character to the *right* of the insertion point. Use this key to delete text to the right of your insertion point. Look for a key labeled *Del* or *Delete*.

CAUTION

If you hold down the Backspace or Delete key rather than pressing it just once or twice, WordPerfect starts erasing at a furious rate. You often end up deleting a lot more than you wanted. Don't hold down these keys unless you've got tons of text to erase.

TIP

As you begin editing your text, keep this in mind: computers are fickle, temperamental, and not to be trusted. If the power goes out and you haven't saved your changes recently, you lose all the editing you've done since the last time you saved. And, as most editors will tell you, it's actually harder to re-edit something than rewrite it. Save often. It doesn't take much time. Just choose **File**, **Save**. Or choose the Save button on the Power Bar (it looks like a little disk with an arrow pointing toward it). Or just press Ctrl+S. Whatever suits your fancy.

Moving, Copying, and Removing Big Chunks of Text

If you don't like the text you've written, delete it. If you don't like where it is, move it. If you like what you've written so much you want a copy of it somewhere else, make multiple copies. WordPerfect makes all of these tasks easy. You *select* the text you want to copy, move or get rid of; then you copy, move, or delete it.

Selecting Text (The electronic highlighter)

The first step in deleting a big chunk of text, or copying or moving text, is *selecting*. Selecting is the WordPerfect equivalent of taking a highlight marker and drawing through text. Once you've marked the text, it's easy to tell WordPerfect what to do next.

39

TIP

As you use WordPerfect, you'll find that you select text to make it bold or italic, to change how big the text is, to center it between margins, or to print a chunk of text. You can do tons of stuff with selected text—more than I have the time or energy to write.

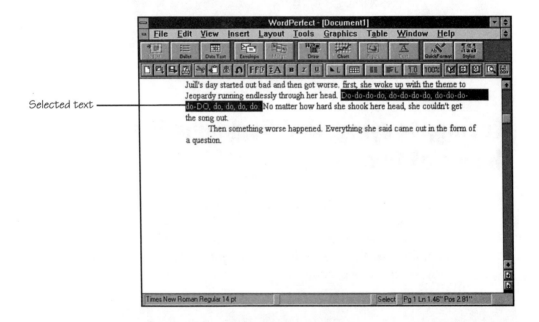

Selected text

Selection selections

✔ The most common way of selecting text is to use your mouse. Click—and hold down the mouse button—at the place you want the selection to begin. Drag the mouse to where you want the selection to end. As you drag, the text becomes highlighted.

✔ Impress your friends by trying this nifty trick: click the insertion point at the beginning of where you want the selection. Then move your mouse pointer to where you want the selection to end. Press and hold the Shift key, and then click the mouse button.

✔ If you want to select a certain word, double-click anywhere on the word.

✔ If you want to select a sentence, *triple-*click (yes, that's right, click three times) anywhere in the sentence.

✔ To select a whole paragraph, click *four* times anywhere in that paragraph (a quadruple click).

✔ If you want to keep your hands on the keyboard, you can select text in almost the same way you move the insertion point. Move the insertion point to where you want to start selecting text; then press and hold down the Shift key. While still holding down the Shift key, use the normal insertion point keys (the arrows and so forth) to move your cursor to the end of the selection.

Deleting the Selection

Once you've selected the text you want to get rid of, getting rid of it is pretty easy. Just press Backspace or Delete, and the marked text disappears.

Deletion fascination

✔ If you want to replace the selected text with new text, just start typing the new text. As soon as you press the first letter, the old selected text disappears, replaced by your new text.

continues

✔ If you change your mind and decide that you didn't want to delete the text after all, move the insertion point to where you want the text. Then choose **E**dit, U**n**delete. Your deleted text reappears, highlighted, and the Undelete dialog box appears. Choose **R**estore to restore the most recently deleted text.

✔ WordPerfect remembers your three most recent deletions. If you block and delete a paragraph, then move down a couple of lines and delete a word, then move down to the bottom of the document and erase the whole last page, you haven't really lost anything. You can get back any of those three deletions. Move your insertion point to where you want the text. Choose **E**dit, U**n**delete; then choose **P**revious until the text you want appears. Choose **R**estore to bring back the text.

✔ You can also use the Undo feature to bring back text you've just deleted—but you've got to use it *immediately* after you make the deletion. To use Undo, press Ctrl+Z (or choose **E**dit, **U**ndo, if you'd rather use menus). The deleted text jumps back right where it was.

Moving Text

As you write documents, you'll probably notice from time to time that a certain sentence would make more sense a couple of paragraphs later, or your introduction works better as a conclusion. And hey, wouldn't point C be clearer if it came between points A and B?

WordPerfect lets you freely move blocks of text. Here's how:

1. Select the text you want to move.

2. Choose **E**dit, **C**ut. Or you can skip this step by clicking the Cut button in the Power Bar.

The block of text disappears. This is called *cutting* because you snipped a chunk of text right out of your document—just as if you had used scissors. That text is now silently lurking in the dark recesses of your computer's memory, waiting for you to need it again.

3. Move the cursor to where you want to insert the block of text.

4. Pull down the Edit menu, and then choose **P**aste. Or skip this step by clicking the Paste button in the Power Bar.

The block of text is pasted to its new place.

Checklist

✔ WordPerfect holds your text in its memory until you cut another block of text or exit WordPerfect. Make sure that you paste (put) the text into a new position in the document before you cut more text or exit WordPerfect. If you don't, the text will be gone forever.

✔ After you've cut text, you can paste it any number of times into as many places as you like. To paste text again, just pull down the Edit menu and choose **P**aste.

✔ You may need to go to the beginning or end of the pasted text and put in some spaces or hard returns (which you make by pressing Enter) to make it look right.

✔ You'll find you use these editing tools all the time, so take the time to learn the shortcut keys: press Ctrl+X to cut and press Ctrl+V to paste.

Copy-Cat Text

Suppose that you want to use the same text more than once. You want the original to stay where it is, but you want to use that same block of text again somewhere else. That's called *copying and pasting*, and this is how you do it:

1. Select the text you want to copy.

2. Pull down the Edit menu, and then choose **Copy**. Or skip this step by clicking the Copy button on the Power Bar.

The highlighting disappears, but a copy of the block is safely tucked away in WordPerfect's memory.

3. Move the cursor to where you want to place a copy of your block of text.

4. Pull down the Edit menu, and then choose **Paste**. Or skip this step by clicking the Paste button in the Power Bar.

The copy of your selected text appears.

Checklist

✔ WordPerfect holds your text in its memory until you copy or cut another block of text or exit WordPerfect. Make sure that you paste (put) the text into a new position in the document before you exit WordPerfect. If you don't, the text will be gone forever.

✔ After you've copied text, you can paste it any number of times into as many places as you like. To paste text again, choose **Edit Paste**.

✔ You may need to go to the beginning or end of the pasted text and put in some spaces or hard returns (which you make by pressing Enter) to make it look right.

✔ If you plan to do a lot of copying, learn the shortcut keystroke so that you don't always have to use the menus. To copy blocked text, press Ctrl+C. To paste the text, press Ctrl+V.

Dragging-and-Dropping

The Cut, Copy, and Paste features in WordPerfect are as handy as can be, but they can also be a little bit cumbersome to work with—especially when you just want to move a tiny amount of text a little distance. First select the text, then copy or cut it, then move the insertion point, and then paste the text. Whew! It's almost easier to retype it. WordPerfect's drag-and-drop feature helps eliminate some of those steps. This feature is great for moving a word, sentence, or paragraph to a different place on-screen. Here's how to use it:

1. Use the mouse to select the text you want to move.

2. Move the mouse pointer so that it's pointing somewhere in the selected text.

3. Click and hold the mouse button, and then move the mouse pointer so that it's where you want to move the selected text.

When you click the mouse, the mouse pointer changes shape, letting you know that drag-and-drop is in effect.

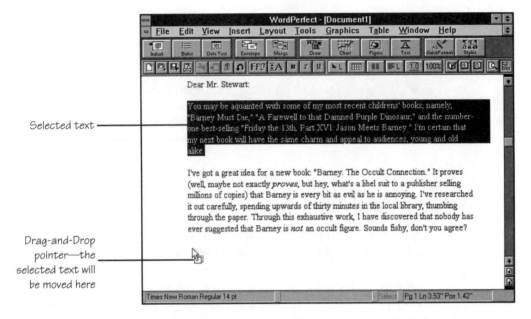

Selected text ───

Dear Mr. Stewart:

You may be aquainted with some of my most recent childrens' books, namely, "Barney Must Die," "A Farewell to that Damned Purple Dinosaur," and the number-one best-selling "Friday the 13th, Part XVI: Jason Meets Barney." I'm certain that my next book will have the same charm and appeal to audiences, young and old alike.

I've got a great idea for a new book: "Barney: The Occult Connection." It proves (well, maybe not exactly *proves*, but hey, what's a libel suit to a publisher selling millions of copies) that Barney is every bit as evil as he is annoying. I've researched it out carefully, spending upwards of thirty minutes in the local library, thumbing through the paper. Through this exhaustive work, I have discovered that nobody has ever suggested that Barney is *not* an occult figure. Sounds fishy, don't you agree?

Drag-and-Drop
pointer—the ───
selected text will
be moved here

4. Release the mouse button.

The selected text is moved from its old location to the new one.

Checklist

✔ You can also use drag-and-drop to make a copy of text that you want to use more than once in the document. Follow the preceding steps, but after step 2, press and hold down the Ctrl key. Keep pressing Ctrl until after you release the mouse button in step 4. The selected text remains where it was, but a copy appears where you release the mouse button.

✔ If you start dragging text and then decide that you don't want to move it after all, move the mouse pointer so that it's pointing somewhere in the blocked text; then let go of the mouse button. The blocked text won't be moved or copied. You can deselect the text by clicking the mouse button somewhere on-screen or by pressing a cursor key.

✔ If you drag-and-drop some text and then decide you don't like it in its new place, pull down the Edit menu and choose Undo. The text goes back to where it was before you started.

✔ Drag-and-drop is best for moving and copying small amounts of text—no more than a couple of paragraphs—across small distances. If you need to move a bigger chunk of text, use Cut, Copy, and Paste.

CHAPTER 3

Formatting Fundamentals

IN A NUTSHELL

▼ Center text

▼ Align text along the right margin

▼ Put today's date in the document

▼ Put an automatically updating date in the document

▼ Add emphasis to your text by making it bold, underlined, or italic

▼ Choose exotic, exciting new fonts

▼ Use tabs and indents

▼ Change the line spacing

▼ Use Quick Format to make your documents consistent

▼ Divide pages

Wow. What a list of topics. This chapter has just about all the features you'll use on a day-to-day basis to make your documents look good. These kinds of changes are called *formatting*. After you master these tricks, you can easily fake your way to a nice-looking letter or report.

Centering Text (Stuck in the middle with you)

If you ever had to center a line of text using a typewriter, you'll be pleased to know that WordPerfect will not make you participate in the same kinds of mathematical gymnastics. In fact, telling WordPerfect to center a title is simple.

Centering One Line

To center only one line, move the insertion point to the beginning of the line you want centered—it can be a blank line or one you've typed already. Choose Layout, Line, and then choose **Center** from the mini-menu that pops out. Your text— or the insertion point, if you're working on a blank line—jumps to the middle of the line. If you're working on a new line, type the text you want centered. As you type, the line automatically adjusts so that the text stays centered. You can edit the line later and it will *still* stay centered.

Checklist

✔ This method doesn't work with text that's more than one line long. If you type so much that the insertion point moves to the next line, neither line will be centered. If you want to center a bunch of lines, read the next section, "Centering a Bunch of Lines."

✔ If you consider yourself a master of the function keys, you can press Shift+F7 to turn on Center. Good luck remembering that.

"I HATE THIS!"

I have to squint to make the text look centered!

The Center feature doesn't center your text between the left and right edges of the page. Instead, WordPerfect centers text between the left and right margins. What's the difference? Well, if your left and right margins are the same size—each one inch, for example—there's no real difference. If your margins are different—say you have a left margin of three inches and a right margin of one-half inch—the center between your margins is different from the center between the edges of the page. Your "centered" text won't look centered at all. What does all this mean? If you're going to use Center, you should have even-sized margins.

Centering a Bunch of Lines

Sometimes a title has several lines and you want them all centered. Move your insertion point to the beginning of the first line you want centered; then follow these steps:

1. Choose Layout, Justification, Center. Or skip this step by choosing the Justification pop-up menu on the Power Bar, and then choosing Center from that menu.

The insertion point jumps to the middle of the line, if it's in a blank line. If your insertion point is at the beginning of text you've already typed, everything after the insertion point is centered.

2. If you want to type new centered text, type it now.

Press Enter at the end of each line you want centered. Or, if you like, just type away. Either way, each line will be centered.

3. Move your insertion point so that it's after the last line you want centered. Or, if you're typing new centered text, after you type the last line you want centered, press Enter to go to the next line.

4. Choose Layout, Justification, Left. Or skip this step by choosing the Justification pop-up menu on the Power Bar, and then choosing Left from that menu.

Aligning Text at the Right Margin

Many business-letter writing styles call for the date to appear at the right margin. In WordPerfect, text aligned on the right margin is called *flush right*. This section tells you how to make text line up along the right margin.

Making One Line Flush Right

To align one line at the right margin, move the insertion point to a new line. This line is where you want to place the right-aligned text. Next choose Layout, Line, Flush Right. The insertion point jumps to the right side of the screen, showing you that it's ready for you to type the text.

Type the text. Notice that as you type, the insertion point stays at the right side of the screen, and text you already typed moves left. In other words, whatever you last typed is always up against the right margin.

Press Enter to go to a new line. The insertion point jumps back to the left side of the screen.

✔ To turn on Flush Right quickly, press Alt+F7.

✔ The text you type shouldn't be more than one line long. If it is, the second line won't be flush with the right margin. If you need to make more than one line flush with the right margin, read "Aligning Lots of Lines," which—for your comfort and convenience—is the very next section in this chapter.

EXPERTS ONLY

Alignment combo

You might someday want a line with some text on the left side, some in the center, and some on the right, like this:

This is left   This is center   This is right

You can do this by using the Center and Flush Right features together. Move your insertion point to a new line; then type the text you want on the left side of the page. Next, choose Layout, Line, Center, and type the text you want in the center. Finally, choose Layout, Line, Flush Right, and type the text you want on the right. When you finish, press Enter to go to a new line.

Aligning Lots of Lines

You can make several rows of text line up on the right margin. Just use the Right Justify feature. Move the insertion point to the first line you want against the right margin. Choose Layout, Justification, **R**ight; or just choose the Justification pop-up menu from the Power Bar, and choose Right from that menu.

Type the lines you want along the right margin, press Enter to go to a blank line, and then choose Layout, Justification, **L**eft to return to normal.

TIP

You can make existing text line up on the right margin easily. Just select the text, and then choose Layout, Justification, Right.

Putting the Date in Your Document

No need to look at that wall calendar any time you need to put the date in your document. WordPerfect has a feature that plops the date in as fast as you can say "What day is this?" You can put in today's date, or you can put in a special date code that automatically updates itself every time you open the document.

What Day Is It?

When you write a letter or report, you usually want to include the current date. That way, if you ever open the document again, you can see when you wrote the letter.

To insert the current date into your document, first move the insertion point to where you want the date to appear—you might want to turn on Flush Right, for example, (which is described earlier in this chapter). Next, choose Insert, Date, and then choose Date Text from the Date submenu. Or you can skip these steps by clicking the Date Text button on the Button Bar. Either way, the date zips into your document, in this format:

October 15, 1993

"I HATE THIS!"

January 1, 1980. Am I in a time warp?

If the wrong date appears, your computer's clock needs to be set. Find someone who's not afraid to brave the dangers of the Windows Control Panel and ask this person to fix your computer's clock. (Computer time is handled by your computer, not by WordPerfect.)

After you insert the date using this technique, the date is just normal text. You can edit it or delete it just as you would any other text in your document.

Inserting a Date that Automatically Updates

WordPerfect lets you insert a date that updates every time you use the document. This little feature might come in handy on a report or memo you are writing. You want the date you *finish* the document to show up—not the date you started it.

When you want an auto-updating date, move the insertion point to where the date should go. Choose Insert, Date, Date Code. The date appears (in the October 15, 1993 format). This date updates itself any time you open or print this document.

✔ WordPerfect uses the computer's clock to figure out the date. If the wrong date appears, find someone familiar with updating the computer's clock to set the proper date for you.

✔ Although this date *looks* like regular text, it's really a special computer code. You can't edit the automatically updating date. To delete it, move your insertion point so that it's right after the date, and then press Backspace once.

Adding Emphasis to Your Text (Make words scream for attention!)

One of the biggest disappointments of the written word is that the reader can't see hand and facial gestures. As I write this book, I'm waving my hands about and grimacing and occasionally sticking out my tongue. And you can't see any of it. What a shame.

But you do have **boldface**, <u>underline</u>, and *italic* to help you add special emphasis to important words. Here's how you type a word—either bold, underline, or italic—that stands out from the crowd:

1. Move the insertion point to where you want to type the emphasized text.

2. Depending on whether you want bold, underline, or italic, press one of the following keystrokes, or click the button in the Power Bar:

✔ Press Ctrl+B to make text **bold**

✔ Press Ctrl+U to make text <u>underlined</u>

✔ Press Ctrl+I to make text *italic*

3. Type the text you want emphasized.

The text appears, emphasized the way you chose.

4. Turn off the text emphasizer by pressing the same key or clicking the same button you used to turn it on.

TIP

You can add emphasis to existing text. Select the text; then press Ctrl+B (for bold), Ctrl+I (for italic), or Ctrl+U (for underline).

After you know how to use these emphasis tricks, you'll be tempted to use them all the time and in combination. Don't. Too much emphasis defeats the purpose and makes your text look hyperactive.

Giving Your Documents a Font Lift

Back in the old days, when dinosaurs walked the earth and the IBM Selectric typewriter reigned supreme, the part of the machine that actually struck the page was a little metal ball covered with letters and

numbers. If you wanted your documents to have a different look, you could remove one ball and stick in a different one. The different balls had the same letters on them, but the letters looked different.

That's the idea behind computer *fonts*. You always have the same letters and numbers available, but you can give those letters and numbers a different look.

With a computer, however, it's easy to change the font in your documents. Here are some different fonts:

Helve

Hobo

Bodoni

S

WordPerfect comes with some fonts, and you may have others that come with Windows and that are installed on your printer.

Choosing a Font

Here's how you choose a new font:

1. Move the insertion point to where you want the new font to begin.

This new font will apply from your insertion point to the end of the document—or until you change the font again. If you want the font in effect for the whole document, press Ctrl+Home to move the insertion point to the beginning of the document.

2. Choose Layout, Font. The Font dialog box appears.

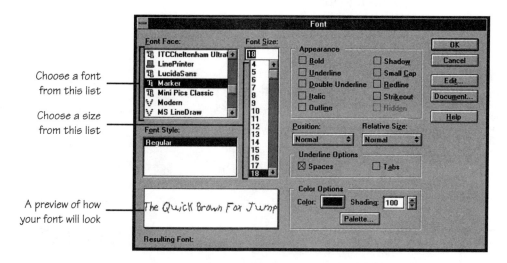

Choose a font from this list

Choose a size from this list

A preview of how your font will look

Your list of fonts might contain only six or seven fonts—or it might contain dozens. It all depends on your printer. You may need to scroll through the list to see all your fonts.

3. Select the font you want from the Font Face list box.

TIP

Any time you highlight a font, the Resulting Font box gives you a preview of how it will look when printed. This helps take the guesswork out of choosing a font.

4. Select a size from the Font Size list box—the bigger the number, the bigger the font. Use **12** for normal-size text, **24** for titles, or **36** for really big, half-inch-high titles. You also can type larger or smaller numbers. Press Enter when you've typed the number you want.

The Resulting Font box shows how large the font will be—if the size fits into that box.

5. Choose OK to close the dialog box and accept the font.

TIP

One size fits all

Not all fonts *let* you choose just any size. These fonts come in just one or two sizes. When this is the case, you have to pick one of the numbers listed in the Font **S**ize list box. If you need a larger font, use one of the fonts that can be sized— WordPerfect comes with a few.

BUZZWORDS

POINT

A measurement, like inches, but much smaller. There are 72 points per inch. So, a half-inch-tall font is 36 points.

Pontificating on fonts

✔ When the list of fonts appears, the font you're currently using is automatically highlighted.

✔ If you are in the Font dialog box and decide you don't want to se- lect a new font after all, choose Cancel to return to your document screen.

✔ To change the font for only part of a document, select the text you want to change and follow steps 2 through 5 in this section.

✔ Experiment with mixing fonts before you use them in documents. Some font combinations work well; others can make you dizzy.

✔ You can add emphasis to your text at the same time you're changing your font. Before you choose OK in the dialog box, check any of the text emphasizers in the Appearance area.

CAUTION

After you become accustomed to the Font feature, you'll be tempted to use it all over the place. If you use too many fonts in a document, your text will look like one of those anonymous threats people tie to bricks and throw through windows.

EXPERTS ONLY

Power fonts for power users using the Power Bar

You can use the Power Bar to change fonts. The only problem is that you don't get the Resulting Font box—like the one in the Font dialog box—to preview how the font will look. So, you'll probably want to use the Power Bar to choose a font only when you already know what the font looks like and how big it will look in the size you choose.

To choose a font from the Power Bar, move your insertion point to where you want the font to begin (or select the text you want to change to the new font); then click the Font button. A menu pops up with a list of your fonts. Click the font you want. The menu disappears, and that new font takes effect.

Set the size of the font by clicking the Font Size button in the Power Bar. You can then either click the font size you want, or type the point size you want and press Enter. Either technique changes the font size.

TIP

Secret Bonus Tip: You can bring up the Font dialog box by double-clicking either the Font or Font Size button in the Power Bar.

Using Tabs and Indents

To make a document more readable, tabs show where paragraphs begin. You can add tabs by pressing the Tab key, or you can let WordPerfect add them automatically. To call attention to a particular paragraph, use the Indent feature, which makes the whole paragraph move farther to the right.

Tabbing

When you want the first line in a paragraph to start a bit farther to the right than the rest of the paragraph, just press Tab. Then type the paragraph. If you already typed the paragraph, move the insertion point to the beginning of the paragraph and press Tab.

Checklist

✔ If you want the first line indented even more, press Tab twice—or as many times as you want.

✔ Don't press Tab at the beginning of each line when you want an indented paragraph. The Indent feature lets you create indented paragraphs with a lot less hassle.

✔ By default, each time you press Tab, your insertion point moves one-half inch. You can change this distance; read the "Changing Tab Stops" section in Chapter 13.

Automatic Tabbing

If you plan to have a tab at the beginning of each paragraph throughout your entire document, WordPerfect can put the tabs in for you. You just press Enter at the end of each paragraph, and WordPerfect indents the first line of your paragraph. Follow these steps:

1. Move the insertion point to the beginning of where you want each paragraph to start with a tab.

The auto-indent feature applies from the position of the insertion point when you turn on auto-indent.

2. Choose Layout, Paragraph, Format.

The Paragraph Format dialog box appears, with 0" already selected in the First Line Indent measurement box.

Type how much
of a first-line indent
you want here

A preview of your first
line indent shows here

Paragraph Format		
First Line Indent: 0"		OK
Spacing Between Paragraphs: 1		Cancel
Paragraph Adjustments		Clear All
Left Margin Adjustment: 0"		Help
Right Margin Adjustment: 0"		

3. Type the amount of space (in inches) that you want the first line of each paragraph to be indented; then choose OK. Or click the up- and down-arrow buttons beside the text box until you have the number you want.

Because the standard tab distance in WordPerfect is one-half inch, you may want to type **0.5**. One-quarter inch also looks good, so you may want to use **0.25**. It's up to you. As you type the number, the sample page at the right side of the dialog box gives you some idea of how your indented paragraphs will look on the page.

After you choose OK, the dialog box disappears. From this point on in the document, the first line in each of your paragraphs will be automatically indented.

TIP

You can use this technique on documents that already exist, too. Just follow the steps, and the first line of existing paragraphs will indent automatically.

Indenting a Paragraph

It's always impressive to quote an expert when you need to give your opinion some backing:

> Dr. Spock agrees that you should not swing a toddler around by his ankles after he has eaten an entire bag of Iced Animal Cookies.

When a quotation is more than three lines long, it belongs in a paragraph of its own. The entire paragraph should be indented to set it apart from regular text.

 To indent a paragraph, move the insertion point to where the paragraph will begin. (If you already typed the paragraph, move the insertion point to the beginning of it.) Choose Layout, Paragraph, Indent to make the whole paragraph jump one-half inch to the right. Or to indent the faster-but-harder-to-remember way, just press F7. The third—possibly easiest—way is to just click the Indent button on the Button Bar.

Checklist

✔ To indent farther to the right, follow the steps for indenting more than once. You can get a good idea of where the left side of the paragraph will be by looking at the Pos measurement in the status line.

✔ You can indent both the left and right sides of a paragraph. Choose Layout, Paragraph, Double Indent.

EXPERTS ONLY

Hangin' 'em high

Once in a while, you may want to indent everything but the first line of a paragraph. This is called a *hanging indent*, and it is useful for bibliographies.

To make a hanging indent, move the insertion point to the beginning of the paragraph, choose Layout, Paragraph, Hanging Indent. Here's how it will look:

Spock, Dr. "The Dangers of the Swinging Toddlers and Iced Animal Cookies." *Pediatric Care*, no. 7 (July 1988): 12-63.

TIP

To make the headings in your document stand out from the rest of the text, try the Margin Release technique. Choose Layout, Paragraph, Back Tab. Type the heading, and then press Enter. You might also want to call attention to the heading by giving it a large point size and making it bold.

Changing Line Spacing

You may have a 9-page report that needs to be 10 pages. You can either go through the report, adding lots of adjectives and maybe a couple of witty anecdotes, or you can take the easy way out—increasing the line spacing. You also can try decreasing the line spacing to fit more on a page. Here's how you change line spacing:

1. Move the insertion point to where you want to change line spacing.

To change the line spacing right from the beginning of the document, press Ctrl+Home. To change line spacing starting with a certain paragraph, move the insertion point to the beginning of that paragraph.

2. Choose Layout, Line, Spacing to go to the Line Spacing dialog box.

1 should already be selected in the Spacing text box.

3. Type the new spacing number, and press Enter.

Type numbers, like **2** for double spacing and **3** for triple spacing. You can also use decimals, like **1.5, 2.2, 1.18**, and so forth. (You can even use fractions, like **1 3/4**, but that's usually more trouble

than it's worth.) If you want, you can click the up- and down-arrow buttons beside the text box to change the spacing. As you change the spacing, the preview page gives you an idea of how your text looks on the page.

4. Choose OK to return to the document screen.

Your new line spacing shows on-screen.

TIP

You can have more than one line spacing change in a document. Each line spacing change stays in effect from where you make the change until the end of the document—or until the next line spacing change.

It Just Keeps Formatting and Formatting and Formatting... (Using Quick Format)

You want to impress your boss with a report you're working on (after all, your yearly review is coming up), so you take the time to set up gorgeous headings—complete with font and size changes, as well as bold and italic. The problem is, setting up just *one* of those headings takes a long time. You're not looking forward to making those formatting changes to each and every one of those headings. Personally, even the *thought* of this much work makes me want to take the rest of the day off.

Well, good news. After you make a formatting change to some text in WordPerfect, it's incredibly easy to apply those changes to other text. You use WordPerfect's Quick Formatting feature.

When you made some formatting changes to text in part of your document and want to make the same kind of changes to other text in your document, follow these steps:

1. Move the insertion point so that it's anywhere inside the text that you already made the formatting changes to.

That's the text you've *already* made the changes to, okay? Not the text you're *going* to make changes to.

2. Choose Layout, Quick Format. Or you can skip this step by clicking the QuickFormat button on the Button Bar.

The Quick Format dialog box pops up, telling you all kinds of stuff you don't need to know. You'll probably read this dialog box once, and then wish you hadn't.

3. Choose OK.

The dialog box goes away and your mouse pointer turns into something that looks like a paint roller and an I-beam.

4. Using the mouse pointer/paint roller/weird goober icon thingy, select the text you want to be formatted.

As soon as you let go of the mouse button, the selected text is formatted so that it's the same as the text you had the insertion point in back in step 1.

5. Repeat step 4 as often as you like, for any text you want formatted in the same way.

6. Choose Layout, Quick Format, or choose the QuickFormat Button Bar button to turn off Quick Format.

TIP

There's a way you can skip step 3 in the preceding steps. In step 1, instead of just moving your insertion point so that it's in the text you want to pattern other text after, select that text. Then when you follow step 2, that pesky dialog box doesn't appear. You can skip step 3 and begin using Quick Format right away.

Awright, Break It Up! (Dividing pages)

After you type for a while, you fill up the screen (unless you're typing something remarkably short, like the New Year's resolutions you stuck to). At that point, the text you wrote earlier moves off the top of the screen and makes room for new words at the bottom of the screen. WordPerfect can tell when the page you're working on doesn't have any more space, and it then gives you a new page. As you fill up each page, a new line appears, signaling that you have begun a new page.

Sometimes you'll want to end a page before it's full of text—for example, you may have created a title page or you may want to end a book chapter. You can repeatedly press the Enter key until a page break appears, but this method is cumbersome and unnecessary. Besides, it can cause problems later.

A better method is to choose **Insert**, **P**age Break; or, if you're good at remembering keystrokes, press Ctrl+Enter. A page break appears at the position of the insertion point.

BUZZWORDS

HARD AND SOFT PAGE BREAKS

When you create a page break yourself, it's called a *hard page break*. When WordPerfect decides that you have enough text on one page and it's time for another, that's called a *soft page break*. The location of soft page breaks changes as you add and delete text so that the page contains the same number of lines. Hard page breaks, on the other hand, do not change when text is added or deleted; the page always ends at the position of the page break you insert, no matter how few lines of text are on the page. Unless you have a plenty special reason for using a hard page break, you're best off letting WordPerfect decide where to end pages.

CHAPTER 4

Printing
(Forget about the Paperless Office)

IN A NUTSHELL

- ▼ Get your printer ready
- ▼ Preview your document
- ▼ Print the whole document
- ▼ Print only one page
- ▼ Print some pages but skip others
- ▼ Print selected text
- ▼ Print several copies of your document
- ▼ What to do when the document won't print

Here we are at the heart and soul of why you use WordPerfect. After climbing mountains of files, fighting through swarms of editing techniques, and subduing formidable formatting features, you're at the point where it finally becomes clear why you spend all those thankless hours at the keyboard.

And what is this end-all and be-all of WordPerfect? Printing. Okay, after all the high-adventure talk in the last paragraph, printing may sound a little anticlimactic. The fact remains, though, that the main reason you use WordPerfect is to get your words onto paper. This chapter shows you how.

Is Your Printer Ready to Print?

From your viewpoint, printing with a typewriter might seem infinitely easier than printing with a computer. With a typewriter, you punch a key, you get a character. But things *will* be easier with a computer after you print that first document and figure out how to set up everything. (Say this with your fingers crossed.)

The first step is to make sure your printer is ready to go. This first step includes several substeps:

✔ Make sure that the printer is turned on and is on-line. (To put a printer on-line, press the On Line button on the printer's panel so that the On Line light is lit. Your printer will probably be on-line when you turn it on.)

✔ Check that the printer has paper in it. If you have a laser printer (these printers look like copy machines), just put paper in the tray and slide the tray into the printer. If you have a dot-matrix printer

(these printers look like a big fancy typewriter), you'll have to loop and weave and wind the paper through its proper contortions. Get help from someone in the know, or—if you dare—check your printer documentation (this is not recommended for the faint of heart).

✔ Make sure that the cable between your printer and your computer is firmly plugged into both ends. Or, better yet, get somebody who can make heads or tails of that tangle of wires to do that for you.

How Will My Document Look on Paper? (Sneak preview)

When you type in WordPerfect, you have a pretty good idea how your text is going to look on the printed page. The trouble is, though, you can only see part of one page at a time. Besides, depending on how you have the "view" set, WordPerfect may not show your page numbers, headers, footers, and so forth. In this case, all you see is the text you type—and that's not a lot to go on.

Before you print, you can take a sneak preview of how the document will appear on paper. To preview your document, make sure that the document you want to preview is on-screen. (Chapter 2 is the place to go if you don't know how to open documents.)

To look at a certain page first, move the insertion point to somewhere on that page. Choose **V**iew, **T**wo Page to see a sneak peek of your document.

The **Two Page** feature gives you a snapshot view of how a couple pages of your document look.

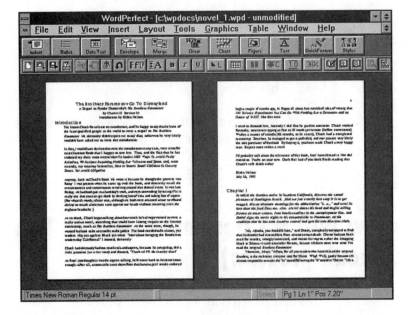

You can move the itsy-bitsy insertion point around normally and make changes here if you like, although you probably won't be able to see the text in your documents well enough to tell exactly what words you're looking at. You mostly use this view to make sure that the general look of the document is good. When you finish looking at the **Two Page** view, choose **View**; then choose either **Draft** or **Page** to return to normal-sized editing.

Checklist

✔ The **Draft** view mode doesn't show headers, footers, page numbers, and all that. Generally, you don't need to see all those elements anyway. It's better to have the space on your screen available for more important things—like the text that you type. I usually return to **Draft** view mode after looking at the document in **Two Page** mode.

✔ The Page mode doesn't hide anything from view. It shows your margins, headers, and footers just as they'll appear on the printed page. If you work in this mode, you'll hardly ever need to use the Two Page mode, since Two Page mode won't have anything new to show you.

Printing the Whole Thing

To print a document, make sure that your printer is ready to go and has enough paper to print the document. Then choose **File**, **Print**. The Print dialog box appears. (You can also bring up the Print dialog box by clicking the Print button on the Power Bar.) **Full Document** is automatically selected, so just choose **Print**.

A box comes up for a moment (or for a minute, or for what seems like forever, depending on how long your document is), telling you WordPerfect is getting ready to print the document. Then WordPerfect goes back to the document screen, and you can go back to work. Meanwhile, your document starts printing.

"I HATE THIS!"

It feels like my computer's wading through molasses!

While your computer is printing your document, it's having to work extra hard. So expect your computer's reaction time to slow down until it's finished printing.

✔ The quick keyboard shortcut for bringing up the Print dialog box is F5.

✔ If you have a mind like a steel trap, you might be able to remember this keyboard shortcut: Ctrl+P. This shortcut prints the current document without your having to mess around with dialog boxes.

✔ To print several documents at once, check out Chapter 9, which tells you how to accomplish this magical feat.

Printing Only One Page

If you need only one page of a document, just print one page of it—no need to waste those extra trees. Move your insertion point to the page you want to print. It doesn't matter where the insertion point is on the page—it can be at the top, bottom, or anywhere in between. You might want to check the page number on the status bar to be sure that you have the insertion point on the right page.

After you're on the right page, choose **File**, **Print** to bring up the Print dialog box. Choose the Current Page button; then choose **Print**. WordPerfect returns you to the document screen and prints the page.

Printing Only Selected Text

Suppose that you don't even want to print an entire page; you just want to print a paragraph or two—or a single sentence. If so, select the text you want to print, and then choose **File**, **Print** to bring up the Print dialog box. Lo and behold, the Selected Text radio button is automatically selected; you just need to choose Print.

TIP

The selected text you print appears in the same place on the page as it would if you printed the entire page. Any page numbers, headers, and footers you have set up also print.

Printing a Few Pages (Picky, picky, picky)

You don't have to print the entire document. In some cases, you may just want to print a few pages.

To print only certain pages from your document, make sure that your printer is set up and that the document is on-screen. Choose **File**, **Print** to make the Print dialog box appear. Then select the **Multiple Pages** button and choose **Print** to bring up the Print Multiple Pages dialog box.

In the Page(s) text box, type the page numbers you want to print, and then choose **Print**. WordPerfect returns to the document screen and only the pages you specified are printed. (This procedure works even if you didn't add page numbers to the document.)

Checklist

✔ To print a sequence of pages, type the first page to be printed, a hyphen, and then the last page to be printed. For example, if you want to print from page three to page eight, type **3-8**.

✔ You also can print individual pages. To do this, type each page number to be printed, separated by commas. For example, to print pages 4, 9, and 12, type **4,9,12**.

continues

✔ You can combine the two ways of printing certain pages. For example, to print pages 1 through 3, as well as pages 8 and 10, type **1-3,8,10**.

✔ To print from the beginning of the document to a certain page, type a hyphen, and then type the last page you want. For example, if you want to print from the beginning of the document to page 13, type **-13**.

✔ To print from a certain page to the end of the document, type the page number followed by a hyphen. For example, to print from page eight to the end of the document, type **8-**.

Printing Several Copies of Your Document (The photocopier effect)

If you like your document enough to want to pass it out to friends, coworkers, and people you meet waiting for the subway, you can print multiple copies.

TIP

If you have a photocopier handy, use it instead of your printer to make the copies. Photocopiers are faster and cost less per page than multiple copies run off your printer. Plus, using a photocopier saves wear and tear on the printer.

Here's how you print several copies of a document:

1. Make sure that the document you want to print is on-screen.

2. Choose File, Print. The Print dialog box appears.

3. In the Number of Copies text box, type the number of copies you want. Or click the up and down arrows beside the text box to set the number.

Don't press Enter or choose Print yet. You still have another decision to make.

4. Click and hold on the button beside Generated by.

A menu appears, with two options: WordPerfect and Printer. If you choose WordPerfect, the copies will be collated, but will come out more slowly. (*Collated* means that one whole copy of the document—from the first to the last page—is printed, and then another whole copy of the document is printed, and so on.)

If you choose Printer, the copies may come out more quickly, but they will not be collated; instead, all the page 1s print, then all the page 2s print, and so on. You have to arrange the documents in the proper order (sort of like when you helped your third-grade teacher assemble stacks of handouts).

5. Choose WordPerfect or Printer.

6. Choose Print.

WordPerfect goes back to the document screen, and your printer begins printing...and printing...and printing....

Problematic Printing

You're finished with that report. What a relief. Now you can print it, mail it, and take off for an early weekend. You send the document to the printer and...nothing. Or maybe something comes out, but it's horribly mangled. What do you do when things go wrong with your printer? Try the suggestions in this section.

If you still can't get things going, find someone who knows about computers and beg that person to help you. Fixing a fussy printer is one of those specialized things that really demands the attention of one of those computer-lover types.

You Can Print, but It Looks All Wrong

If the awful mess that comes out of your printer bears little or no resemblance to the document you just typed, one of two things has probably happened:

✔ If you're using a laser printer that uses font cartridges, someone might have taken out the font cartridge that you need. Find somebody who understands your printer and ask him to put the cartridge you need back into the printer.

✔ If strange symbols and characters print in your document, or if the printer spits out page after page with only a couple of lines on each piece of paper, you probably have the wrong printer driver selected. To determine which printer driver is selected, choose **File**, **Print** to bring up the Print dialog box. Look at the name of the printer in the Current Printer box, which is at the very top of the dialog box. If the name of the printer doesn't match the name of your printer, choose Select. A list of printers appears, and your printer should be

one of them. (If it isn't, find someone who *really* knows WordPerfect and ask him to help you "install a printer driver.") Highlight the printer you are using, choose Select, and then try printing again.

Nothing Prints at All

Hoo boy. Diagnosing the problem when a printer doesn't print at *all* can be a real chore. Try the following solutions in order. After trying each suggestion, try printing again. If you still don't have any luck, call WordPerfect Customer Support. The folks there will be happy to help you work through the problem.

Checklist

✔ Make sure that your printer is on, is on-line, and has paper in it. Also, make sure that the cable that connects your printer to your computer is firmly connected. If you're not sure which cable this is, find somebody who likes to fiddle with computers and ask him.

✔ Leave WordPerfect and try printing from another program. If you can't print from *any* of your programs, there's a problem with either Windows, the printer, the cable, or your computer.

✔ Leave WordPerfect, leave Windows, reset your computer, and then come back into Windows and WordPerfect. This chases away little gremlins that tend to accumulate in computers after they've been on for a while. Try printing the document again.

✔ Turn off your printer, wait for a few seconds, and then turn on the printer again. Sometimes printers can crash, just like your computer does. By turning the thing off and back on, you clear the printer's memory.

CHAPTER 5
Help Me!

IN A NUTSHELL

▼ Look up a topic
▼ Use Help for reminding you how to do things
▼ Get help on the feature you're now using
▼ Let WordPerfect guide you through a task
▼ Go to WordPerfect school

With a program as complex as WordPerfect, you need all the help you can get. After all, it has around 9.3 bazillion features. Not to mention that between menus, mice, function keys, and shortcut keys, there are enough ways to get to any feature that it's nearly impossible to remember *any* of them.

But not to worry. This book will help you safely ignore most of those features and strange access methods. In addition, WordPerfect has the Help feature, which is designed to answer any questions you have while using WordPerfect. You can get an overview of the feature you're currently using, look up how to accomplish certain tasks, and even have WordPerfect give you an interactive lesson. This chapter shows you how.

Look It Up

If you know which feature you need help on, just follow these steps:

1. Choose Help, Search for Help On.

A list of topics appears in a list box, with your insertion point in a text box above the list box. The information you need is almost certainly in that mile-long list, if you dare to look it up.

2. Begin typing the name of the feature or a key word you want help with. (Or just scroll through the list, if you're not in a typing mood.)

If you type key words to the feature, WordPerfect will highlight the closest item to what you've typed. After you've typed the first few letters of the topic, you should be able to see whether it's in the list. Then you can click the topic to highlight it.

3. After the feature you want is highlighted, choose Show Topics to see what Help topics address this word.

"I HATE THIS!"

I can't find what I need!

With such a huge index of topics, you'd think that every possible thing you'd ever need help on would be listed. *Wrong.* Sometimes WordPerfect seems to have cleverly anticipated what you're looking up, then indexed everything *except* what you need. Try thinking of other key words that might have something to do with what you need to look up. Or use this book.

A list of topics appears in the list box in the bottom half of the screen—the list might contain only one or two topics, or it might contain several.

4. Double-click the topic to get the help you want.

The Help screen on that topic appears.

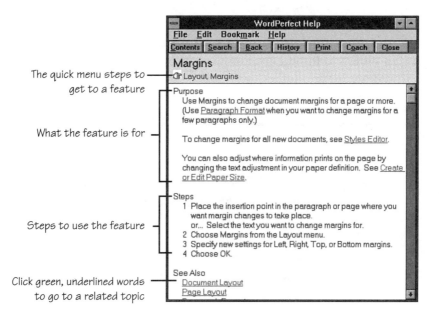

The quick menu steps to get to a feature

What the feature is for

Steps to use the feature

Click green, underlined words to go to a related topic

85

I HATE WORDPERFECT FOR WINDOWS!

Help using Help

✔ There's probably more to the Help topic than will fit on your screen. Use the vertical scroll bar or the down-arrow key to scroll through more of the text.

✔ If you find what you need and want it for reference, choose the **P**rint button at the top of the Help Window. The Help topic prints out.

✔ Below the Help text, you will sometimes find related topics listed. These topics are underlined and are green on most computers. (If you're not using a color computer, just look for the underlined words.) You can click the text to get help for that topic.

✔ That underlined, green text also can be elsewhere in the Help text. Just click it to jump to that topic.

✔ If you jump to a Help topic that turns out to be useless, choose **B**ack. This takes you back to the previous screen.

✔ If you want to look up a new topic, choose Search. The Search dialog box appears, and you can search for a new keyword and topic.

✔ When you're finished with the Help system, choose Close.

TIP

A quick way to exit the Help system is to click in the WordPerfect document window. The Help window disappears. A nice side effect of this trick is that you can return to the Help topic you were looking at by holding down the Alt key and pressing Tab until you see a WordPerfect Help box; once the box appears, you can let go of the Alt key.

Howd'ya Do That?
(Using Help's How Do I feature)

If you've got a question about how to do something, WordPerfect's How Do I feature *might* be able to help you. Say your question is, "How do I number pages in my document?" The How Do I feature could answer your question. If, on the other hand, your question is "How do I get that cute secretary on the fifth floor to notice me?" you'd better ask someone else.

The How Do I feature organizes frequently asked WordPerfect questions in a semi-logical order. You search for a heading, then search for the related topic.

To use WordPerfect's How Do I feature, choose **Help**, **How Do I**. Two windows appear, side-by-side.

Help on the topic you choose

How Do I topics

Use this scroll bar to see more topics

Use this scroll bar to see more Help text

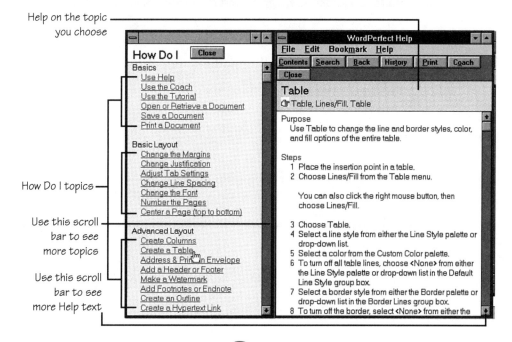

The left window displays a list of topics WordPerfect can describe. Each of the topics is underlined and is probably green. Scroll through this list until you see the topic you want, and then click the topic.

For example, if you wanted to learn about margins, you would bring up the How Do I window, and then look at the topics under Basic Layout. Sure enough, there's a topic named Change the Margins. Of course, this all supposes that you know the difference between *basic* layout and *advanced* Layout, and that you know to find margins under layout in the first place. This feature can be frustrating at times.

Help on the topic you want appears in the right window. Read the text. When you're finished, choose the Close button in the right window. Then choose the Close button in the left window to get back to your document.

Checklist

✔ You can treat the right window like you would any Help screen. For help on how to maneuver in Help screens, read the "Help using Help" checklist in the "Look It Up" section earlier in this chapter.

✔ Once you're done reading the text in one Help topic, you can click another How Do I topic in the left screen to read about another topic.

✔ If you don't have any luck finding the topic you need in the How Do I part of the Help system, try the Look It Up feature explained earlier in this chapter.

EXPERTS ONLY

For the truly curious

WordPerfect has a Help feature for the innately curious—for those who *have* to know what some strange option on a menu is for, or what some weird button means. It's called the What Is feature, and it's easy to use. When you want to know the purpose of some part of WordPerfect, press Shift+F1. The mouse pointer suddenly has a cute little bubble with a question mark inside:

You then click whatever you're interested in learning about. Or, if you're interested in learning about some option in a menu, click and hold on the word in the menu bar, and then drag to the menu option you want to learn about. Don't let go of the mouse button until the topic is highlighted.

When you let go of the mouse button, a Help screen appears, with help on whatever you selected. Now read the text, and then choose the Help window's Close button to go back to the document window.

Anywhere, Anytime

You never know when a WordPerfect dilemma will rear its ugly head. It could be while you're changing your line spacing or deciding where your page numbers should go. You can locate help on the feature you're using

by pressing F1. A box appears with instructions on how to use the feature you're working on. Press Esc when you're finished with the Help box and want to return to your document.

✔ There's probably more to the Help topic than will fit on your screen. Use your down-arrow key to scroll through more of the text.

✔ You will notice that some of the words in the Help text are underlined and a different color—usually green. You can click on these terms to get information on that topic. When you're done, choose Close to leave Help or choose **B**ack to go back to the Help topic you were looking at before.

✔ Some terms in Help have a dotted underline below them. If you click on one of these terms, a definition pops up. Click on the definition to return to the Help screen when you're finished reading the definition.

✔ Most dialog boxes have a **H**elp button. If you want help while you're using that dialog box, just click the button, or press F1—they both lead to the same place.

Hey, Coach!

There are a few things that most people need to do once in a while, like making bulleted lists, creating outlines, and using bold and italic. WordPerfect's Coach feature guides you, step-by-step, through these tasks. To get WordPerfect to coach you, follow these steps:

1. Choose Help, Coach.

A list of tasks appears—these are the things WordPerfect can coach you through. Use your arrow keys to scroll through the list.

2. Double-click one of the items in the list.

A clipboard-looking thing appears on-screen, where the Coach gives you a description of the feature you want to be coached on, and asks what you want to do. You'll then be guided step-by-step through the whole process of using the feature. The Coach will help you choose items from the menu, select the right options in the dialog boxes, and even point out which buttons to press.

TIP

Because WordPerfect has a limited number of Coach topics, you might not find what you need. If you can't find the topic you want, choose Cancel to leave the Coaches dialog box.

A Quick Trip to WordPerfect U

If you're feeling extra-ambitious, you might want to go through some of the interactive tutorials that come with WordPerfect. They take you through some of the same features that you learned in the first part of this book and might help you get a better handle on how WordPerfect works. Follow these steps to get a few hands-on lessons from Professor WordPerfect:

1. Choose Help, Tutorial.

The Tutorial dialog box appears.

2. Double-click on one of the lessons, and follow WordPerfect's instructions.

✔ There are five lessons, and you can start with whichever one you want—you don't have to do them in order.

✔ If you get tired of the lesson, you can leave by choosing the Exit button. A box then appears containing two options: **R**eturn to Lesson or **G**o to Main Menu. To leave the lesson, choose **G**o to Main Menu, and then choose **E**xit Tutorial.

PART II

The On-Line Editorial Assistant

Includes:

CHAPTER 6

Proofreading Your Documents

(Getting It Right)

IN A NUTSHELL

- ▼ Check the spelling in your document
- ▼ Check the spelling in a single page
- ▼ Check the spelling in a block
- ▼ Look up a word's spelling
- ▼ Add new words to WordPerfect's dictionary
- ▼ Find synonyms for words
- ▼ Find antonyms for words
- ▼ Have WordPerfect check your grammar

I HATE WORDPERFECT FOR WINDOWS!

This chapter isn't meant to imply that you are a lousy speller. Just the opposite might be true: you're probably a *great* speller who has won plenty of awards in spelling-bee competitions. However, most of us are lousy spellers, and the few of us who are gifted spellers still make typos. It comes down to this: we all make spelling mistakes.

WordPerfect is a lifesaver when checking for spelling errors. Word-Perfect can look through documents and flag any possible mistakes; then, it lets you decide how to correct them. You also can polish your writing by finding *precisely* the correct word with WordPerfect's Thesaurus. You also can use Grammatik, the grammar checker included with WordPerfect, to wade through a document and point out possible writing mistakes.

"I HATE THIS!"

The work of a proofreader is never finished

WordPerfect does not take the place of a careful proofreader. The spell checker, thesaurus, and grammar checker combined still can't tell you if your writing sounds good. After you finish using WordPerfect's proofreading tools, read your document again—or have someone else take a look at it—to see whether your writing is easy to understand.

Revving Up the Speller

Before you can check your document's spelling, the document must be on-screen; the position of the insertion point doesn't matter. Then follow these steps:

1. Choose **T**ools, Speller. Or, using the mouse, click the Speller button on the Power Bar.

The Speller dialog box appears at the bottom of the screen. It has all kinds of buttons, boxes, and menus, but you don't need to worry about them—at least, not yet.

2. Choose the Start button.

WordPerfect begins chugging away, looking for misspelled words.

When WordPerfect finds an error—or a word it *thinks* is an error—that word is highlighted. The Speller dialog box shows the word that is highlighted and some possible replacements. Your screen looks like this:

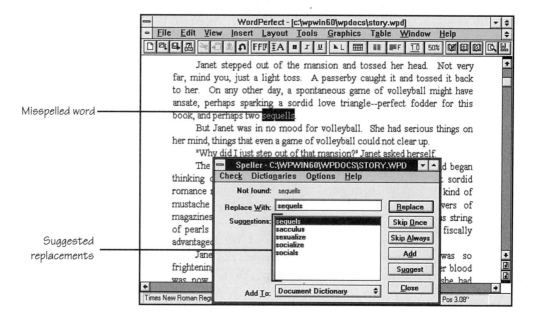

Misspelled word

Suggested replacements

✔ If the correct spelling is in the Suggestions list box, double-click the correct spelling, or just highlight the spelling and choose **R**eplace. You might have to scroll through the list box to find the correct spelling.

✔ WordPerfect doesn't know every word in the English language (or any other language, for that matter). When it comes across a name or a specialized term it doesn't recognize, WordPerfect usually thinks the word is spelled wrong. Choose the A**d**d button to make that word part of your dictionary.

✔ If WordPerfect stops on a misspelled word but doesn't have any suggestions—or none of its suggestions are what you want—move the insertion point to the Replace **W**ith text box. Erase any text already in the box, type the word you want, and then choose **R**eplace.

✔ WordPerfect thinks any word with a number is wrong. If you use words that contain numbers, choose the **O**ptions menu in the Speller dialog box, and then choose Words with **N**umbers to turn off number checking.

✔ If you want to check part of your document—such as a word, sentence, or paragraph—select that text before choosing **T**ools, Speller. Then run the spell check.

✔ If you have the same word twice in a row (such as "up up and away!"), WordPerfect views that as a problem, and brings up a dialog box accusing `Duplicate Words Found`. Choose **C**ontinue if you *meant* to have the same word twice, or choose Delete **2**nd to get rid of the spare.

✔ If a word contains unusual capitalization, such as the first two letters being capitalized, WordPerfect gives you a list of more ordinary capitalization in the Suggestions list box. Double-click one of these, or choose Skip **A**lways if you want the capitalization left the way it is. For example, if you were crazy enough to put a capital letter in the middle of your company name, such as *WordPerfect*, you'd want to leave the capitalization alone.

✔ If you want to stop the spell check before WordPerfect is finished, choose **C**lose.

✔ When WordPerfect has finished, it shows a prompt telling you so and asking whether you want to close the Speller. Choose **Y**es to return to your document.

✔ Make sure you save your document after spell checking so that you don't lose the corrections.

EXPERTS ONLY

Ahhh, skip it

If WordPerfect stops on an unusual word, but you don't want to add the word to the dictionary, choose **S**kip Always. WordPerfect will ignore the word during this spell check. You also can have WordPerfect skip the word once only by choosing Skip **O**nce, but I can't think of any reasons you would want to do that.

"I HATE THIS!"

Their, they're, deer, don't cry

WordPerfect's Speller isn't perfect. There are a couple things it won't do.

✔ WordPerfect's "dictionary" is really nothing more than a long list of words. If you want a definition, you're going to have to get out the old-fashioned paper dictionary and look up the word.

✔ WordPerfect is not a proofreader. When WordPerfect checks your spelling, it looks only for incorrectly spelled words. It has no way of telling whether you used the correct words. If you write "What a pane in the neck," WordPerfect won't see a problem because the word "pane" is spelled correctly. Therefore, use WordPerfect to check spelling, but make sure you *reed* your document carefully *two* make sure it makes *cents*.

Looking Up a Word

There are certain words people simply don't remember how to spell. "Definitely" is *definately* one of them. If you need to write a word that you just don't know how to spell, you can look it up. Here's how:

1. Type your best guess for the word.

If you don't know the correct spelling, take a wild guess.

2. Choose **T**ools, **S**peller. Or click the Speller button on the Power Bar. The Speller dialog box appears.

3. In the Speller dialog box, choose the Check menu, and then choose **W**ord. Choose Start.

WordPerfect will take a couple of guesses at what it thinks you meant to type, shown in the Suggestions list box. One of them will likely be the correct spelling.

4. Choose **C**lose to close the Speller.

TIP

If you really have no idea how part of the word is spelled, just put an asterisk (*) in place of that part. The asterisk means "I'm not sure how this chunk of the word is spelled." Suppose you need to use *hematophagous* (and I hope that you never do) but don't have a clue what comes between the *hem* and the *us*. Type **hem*us** in the Replace With text box. Among several other wildly obscure words, *hematophagous* appears in the Suggestions list box.

Finding the Right Word

If you've ever stared blankly at your computer for ten minutes hoping to think of that ideal word, WordPerfect's Thesaurus might be the perfect brainstorming tool. The Thesaurus lists *synonyms* (words with the same—or at least similar—meaning) for a selected word. This same feature also lists *antonyms* (words with the opposite meaning of the selected word).

To find a synonym or antonym, move the cursor under the word you want to check. Choose **T**ools, **T**hesaurus to bring up the Thesaurus dialog box. You also can click the Thesaurus button in the Power Bar.

A dialog box with three columns appears at the bottom of the screen. The word you're looking up is selected at the top of the screen, and a series of synonyms and antonyms appears in the first column. After the synonyms comes a separator line; then any antonyms are listed. There will probably be more synonyms and antonyms than will fit on the screen, so you can scroll through the column for more words.

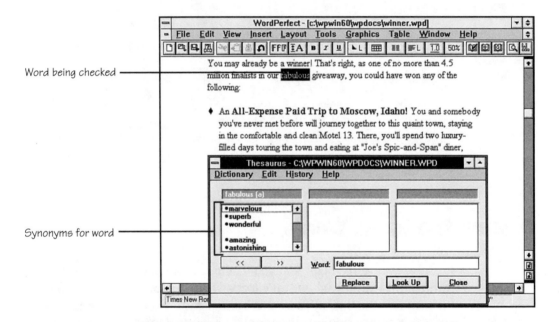

Word being checked

Synonyms for word

"I HATE THIS!"

What's a synonym for "moronic"?

WordPerfect doesn't know synonyms or antonyms for every word. If it doesn't have any suggestions, the Thesaurus dialog box comes up, but there won't be any words in the list boxes. You can look up a different word by typing a word in the **W**ord text box, and then choosing **L**ook Up. Or, if you're completely disgusted with the Thesaurus for not knowing your word, choose **C**lose to get out of the Thesaurus.

Replacing the Word

If you see a word you like better in the replacement list, select it by clicking it; then choose **R**eplace. The Thesaurus box disappears and you can get back to writing.

To leave the Thesaurus without picking any words, choose **C**lose.

CAUTION

Don't take WordPerfect's word for it! If WordPerfect says a word is a synonym for a word you're looking up, but you're not familiar with the word, look up the word in the dictionary. Make sure that it means what you want.

Looking Up Synonyms of the Synonyms

You can look up synonyms—and antonyms—of the words in the Thesaurus columns. Double-click on the word you're interested in: a column containing synonyms and antonyms for the word appears to the right of the column.

Checklist

✔ A festive little "pointing hand" appears by the word you double-click when you look up a synonym of a synonym. This is to remind you which word in the column you've looked up.

✔ If a word doesn't have a dot by it, don't bother looking it up; WordPerfect doesn't have any additional synonyms or antonyms for it.

continues

✔ If you fill up all three columns, you can still look up synonyms. The old columns of synonyms just move off to the left. You can review the old columns by clicking the << button; your old columns of words reappear. You can go right again by clicking the >> button.

✔ If you want to look up a word that isn't in your text, choose **Tools, Thesaurus.** Then click in the Word text box, type the word you want to check for synonyms, and choose Look Up.

Fixin' Yer Grammer

It is often said (*Hey! That's passive voice!*) that grammar is important. It makes sense to frequently use (*Whoa! That's a split infinitive!*) the grammar checker which (*Oops! The correct restrictive pronoun is "that"*) comes with WordPerfect. By using it, your writing can really improve (*There's a dangling modifier*). So, without further ado (*Watch out for those cliches*), let's see how it works.

Grammatik, a grammar checker that comes with WordPerfect, walks you through your document, freely dispensing comments about what a miserable writer you are. Don't use it if you're not in a mood to take advice— Grammatik gives plenty of advice. If you're willing to take the criticism, though, Grammatik can give you some useful pointers. To check your document's grammar, follow these steps:

1. Choose **Tools, Grammatik.** Or just click the Grammatik button on the Power Bar.

    Don't be too concerned that you're about to use a grammar checker that doesn't use the correct spelling of "grammatical." The Grammatik dialog box appears.

2. Choose Start.

Grammatik starts checking your document. When it finds a mistake, it highlights the problem in your document and describes the problem in the dialog box.

Grammar problem

Description of the problem and suggestions for fixing the problem

Replacement box

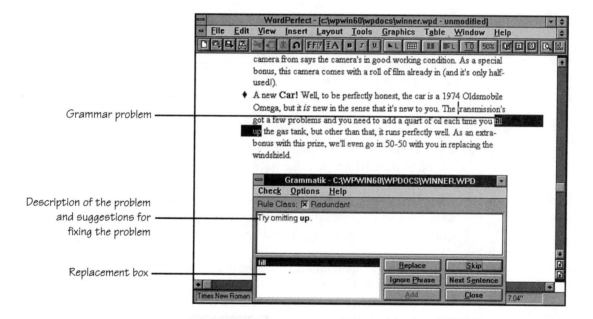

How to cope with Grammatik's nit-picky remarks

✔ Grammatik sometimes provides suggested changes in the Replacement box. If you want to use the replacement, select the replacement and choose **R**eplace.

✔ Usually, Grammatik's suggestions will be general, and you'll have to fix the problem yourself. To do this, click in the document window, make the change, and then click the Resume button to have Grammatik continue.

continues

I HATE WORDPERFECT FOR WINDOWS!

How to cope with Grammatik's nit-picky remarks (continued)

✔ Remember that Grammatik is much more picky than human readers; you don't have to do *everything* the grammar checker suggests. In fact, if you make some of the changes, your writing will start to look incredibly stilted. To skip a problem Grammatik flags, choose Skip.

✔ If Grammatik pesters you about a certain rule over and over, click the check box above the description of the problem. A box appears, telling you that the rule is turned off for the rest of the grammar check. Choose OK. Choose **R**esume to continue checking from there.

✔ If you've had enough before Grammatik is done, choose the **C**lose button to get back to your document.

✔ After Grammatik is finished, it brings up a box asking whether you want to close Grammatik. Look around for a button that says `Hell, Yes!` When you can't find one, just choose **Y**es.

✔ When you close Grammatik, it might bring up a box saying, `You have turned off some rule classes. Do you want to save these changes to a custom writing style?` Choose **N**o.

CHAPTER 7

Finding and Replacing Text

(The WordPerfect Swap Meet)

IN A NUTSHELL

- ▼ Find a word
- ▼ Find formatting "codes"
- ▼ Replace one word or phrase with another—one at a time
- ▼ Replace one word or phrase with another in one fell swoop

You're at the end of a long chapter in your novel and you can't remember the fate of Aunt Matilda. Something happened to mean, old Aunt Matilda somewhere in the chapter, but you can't remember where or what. Did authorities find the dead man in her cellar and give her the electric chair? Or did she escape on her Harley?

WordPerfect's Find feature can help with these types of dilemmas. Instead of reading through the entire chapter, you can use the Find feature to look for specific text—such as *Matilda*.

WordPerfect's companion feature, Replace, is another great editing tool. Suppose your *real* Aunt Matilda calls and says that on second thought, she *is* going to include you in her will. You better change all references from mean, old Aunt Matilda to mean, old Aunt Helga. That's when Replace comes in handy.

Finding Lost Text (The WordPerfect detective agency)

Use Find whenever you need to find a certain word or phrase. The search begins from your insertion point and stops when it finds the text you need. You can search backward or forward through the document.

Here's how you search for specific text:

1. Move the insertion point to wherever you want to begin the search.

Remember that you can search in either of two directions: from the insertion point toward the beginning of the document, or from the insertion point to the end of the document.

TIP

If you want to search through all the text in the document, don't bother moving the insertion point. The checklist in this section shows you how to search through the entire document—without moving the insertion point.

2. Choose Edit, Find.

Find highlights the text you're searching for

Click here to search down

Type the text you want to look for here

Click here to search up

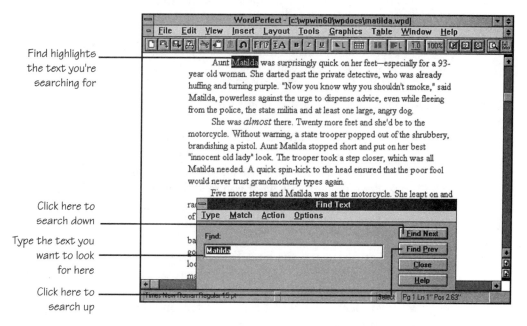

3. Type the word or phrase you want WordPerfect to find.

4. Choose Find Next to make WordPerfect look forward for the text, or choose Find Previous to have WordPerfect look backward.

The text you're searching for is highlighted. From here you can either choose Close to make the dialog box go away or choose Find Next (or Find Previous) to look for another occurrence of the text.

✔ You also can display the Find Text dialog box by pressing F2.

✔ If you want to search through the whole document, follow steps 1 through 3. Next, choose the Options menu in the Find Text dialog box, and then choose **B**egin Find at Top of Document. Choose Find Next each time you want to continue the search.

✔ Normally, if you try to find a word like *car*, WordPerfect stops at any word that contains the letters *car*: *card*, *streetcar*, *reincarnate*, and so on. But what if you only want to find *car*? You choose the Match menu in the Find Text dialog box, and then choose **W**hole Word. Make sure you follow this step before you choose either of the Find buttons. WordPerfect now only stops on the word you're looking for, not other words that contain the word.

✔ If WordPerfect can't find the text you want, a box appears on-screen to tell you so. Choose OK and the box disappears. If you get this box and you're sure the text is there, try again. Make sure that you're typing exactly what you're looking for—don't add any extra spaces or punctuation at the end of the word. If you still get this message, try searching in the other direction.

✔ When you access the Find Text dialog box and text from a previous search appears, just type the new text. The old text disappears.

✔ If you access the Find Text dialog box and then decide you don't want to start a search, choose **C**lose to go back to the document screen.

TIP

If you close the Find Text dialog box and then decide you want to continue the search, just press Shift+F2. WordPerfect jumps to—and highlights—the next instance of the text you last typed in the Find Text dialog box. You can press Shift+F2 over and over to skip quickly from one instance of the word to the next. You can't, however, use this technique to move backward through the document.

EXPERTS ONLY

The case of a sensitive search

When WordPerfect searches for text, it usually matches the text you type to both lowercase and uppercase letters. So, whether you type **nacho**, **Nacho**, **NACHO**, or **NaChO** as your search text, WordPerfect would think *nacho*, *Nacho*, *NACHO*, or anything in between is a match and would stop.

If you want WordPerfect to find an *exact* match of your search text, right down to how you capitalize the text, choose the **Match** menu from the Find Text dialog box, and then choose **Case**. For example, if you type **Frijole** as your search text, WordPerfect will count *Frijole* as a match, but not *frijole*, *FRIJOLE*, *FrIjOLe*, or anything else.

Finding Your Formatting

You also can search for WordPerfect *formatting codes*. If your text is bold, it's because of a code. If you've got a centered title, that's a code, too.

New font? Codes again. Using a different margin? Italics? Tab? They're all codes. WordPerfect has more codes than the FBI, CIA, and Little Orphan Annie, combined.

If you want to search for the next place that bold formatting occurs, choose **Edit**, **Find** to bring up the Find Text dialog box. Now choose the **Match** menu from the Find Text dialog box's menu bar. Choose Codes from the menu to bring up the Codes dialog box, which contains a list of codes.

"I HATE THIS!"

Is this the Russian alphabet?

The codes in the Codes dialog box are in alphabetical order, although the first 20 or so codes have strange ch aracters in front of them that bring them to the top of the list. After you scroll past these strange codes, the rest are alphabetical.

Scroll through the list until you find the code you want, such as **Bold On**. Double-click it (or highlight it and choose Insert), and [Bold On] appears in the Search For text box. You can search for other formatting things, like Tabs, Enters (called HRt in this list, which stands for *Hard Return*), line spacing changes, and so forth. Just scroll through the codes list, highlight the code you want to search for, and choose Select. When you're ready to begin the search, choose the **Close** button in the Codes dialog box, and then choose Find Next (or Find Prev) in the Find Text dialog box.

"I HATE THIS!"

I Can't Find the $#&?!% Code!

WordPerfect has some really strange names for some of its codes; you may not find them where you'd expect. For example, if you want to find the next place you used an Indent in your document, search for a **Hd Left Indent**, not *Indent*.

The best way to figure out what WordPerfect calls some of these codes is to find the feature you want to search for, and then look at it in Reveal Codes, which is discussed in Chapter 13. The code name is usually shown in Reveal Codes.

Using the Replace Feature (Pulling the old switcharoo)

Now to get back in Aunt Matilda's good graces. Every time her name appears in the novel you're writing, you want to replace it with *Helga*. Does this mean you're going to have to read through the whole novel? You don't want to have to comb through every word, looking for *Matilda*, erasing her name every time you see it, and then typing *Helga* in its place.

With the Replace feature, you don't have to. The Replace feature is perfect for making wholesale changes to your documents. You can use it to change every instance of a word or phrase into another, or you can pick and choose.

Follow these steps to replace one word or phrase with a different word or phrase:

1. Move the insertion point to where you want to begin replacing text.

Usually, you'll want to start replacing from the top of the document. If so, you don't have to move the insertion point to the beginning of the document. In just a second you'll see how to make WordPerfect automatically jump to the beginning.

I HATE WORDPERFECT FOR WINDOWS!

2. Choose **E**dit, **R**eplace. The Find and Replace Text dialog box appears.

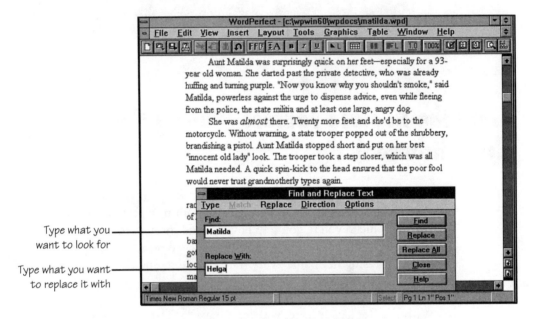

WordPerfect - [c:\wpwin60\wpdocs\matilda.wpd]

File   Edit   View   Insert   Layout   Tools   Graphics   Table   Window   Help

Aunt Matilda was surprisingly quick on her feet—especially for a 93-year old woman. She darted past the private detective, who was already huffing and turning purple. "Now you know why you shouldn't smoke," said Matilda, powerless against the urge to dispense advice, even while fleeing from the police, the state militia and at least one large, angry dog.

She was *almost* there. Twenty more feet and she'd be to the motorcycle. Without warning, a state trooper popped out of the shrubbery, brandishing a pistol. Aunt Matilda stopped short and put on her best "innocent old lady" look. The trooper took a step closer, which was all Matilda needed. A quick spin-kick to the head ensured that the poor fool would never trust grandmotherly types again.

Find and Replace Text

Type   Match   Replace   Direction   Options

Find:
Matilda

Replace With:
Helga

Find
Replace
Replace All
Close
Help

Times New Roman Regular 15 pt   Select   Pg 1 Ln 1" Pos 1"

Type what you want to look for

Type what you want to replace it with

3. Type the text you want to replace in the Find text box. For your novel, you would type **Matilda**, which is the text that needs to be replaced.

Now press Tab to move the insertion point into the Replace **W**ith text box.

4. Type the replacement text in the Replace **W**ith text box.

For your novel, type **Helga**. That's the text you want to insert in place of the text in step 3.

TIP

> If you want the replacing to begin at the top of the document, choose the **O**ptions menu from the Find and Replace Text dialog box, and then choose **B**egin Find at Top of Document.

5. Choose Find.

WordPerfect zooms through your document, looking for the text in the Find text box. When it finds a match, that text is highlighted.

6. If you want to replace the word, choose **R**eplace. If you want to leave the word alone and continue searching, choose **F**ind again.

7. Repeat step 6 until WordPerfect has found all the examples of the text you're looking for.

When WordPerfect has found all the examples of the text you want to replace, a box appears with Not Found.

8. Choose OK, and then choose **C**lose in the Find and Replace Text dialog box.

Checklist

✔ You can also bring up the Find and Replace Text dialog box by pressing Ctrl+F2.

✔ If you want to replace text only within a certain part of your document, select that part of your document before following these steps.

✔ If you look at your document after the Find and Replace is done and notice that something went horribly wrong (you just

continues

replaced all occurrences of the letter *t* with the letter *m* in an important report), choose **E**dit, **U**ndo to return the document to how it was before the Search and Replace.

✔ The Replace feature is terrific for cleaning up irregular capitalization. For example, if you sometimes forgot to capitalize *American*, you can fix the problem in one pass. For the Find text, type the word you forget to capitalize, leaving the whole thing in lowercase (**american**). For the Replace With text, type the word with its correct capitalization (**American**). Choose Replace **A**ll to make the replacements all at once.

✔ Your documents will look their best if you have only one space at the end of each sentence. (Two spaces at the end of each sentence went out with the typewriter.) You can get rid of those habitual extra spaces by using the Replace feature. For the Find text, press the space bar twice. For the Replace With text, press the space bar once. Choose Replace **A**ll to make the replacements all at once.

✔ You can use the Replace feature to remove all occurrences of a word or phrase and replace the word or phrase with nothing. In the Find text box, type the text you want to get rid of; make sure that the Replace With text box contains no text; and then choose **F**ind, **R**eplace or Replace **A**ll. You might expect a gaping hole where your text used to be, but WordPerfect actually closes this gap.

✔ You can have the Search and Replace start from your insertion point and work toward the beginning of the document, if you like. Just choose **D**irection, **B**ackward from the menu in the Find and Replace dialog box.

TIP

If you're absolutely sure that you want to replace each and every instance of one word or phrase with another, use the devil-may-care Replace All button. Once you've typed the Find text and the Replace With text, choose Replace All. WordPerfect rockets through the document, making all the changes. When it's done, a box comes up telling you all matching text has been replaced. Choose OK, and then choose Close.

CHAPTER 8
Cool Editing Tools

IN A NUTSHELL

▼ Use the Power Bar

▼ Use the Button Bar

▼ Customize the Button Bar

▼ See your document in draft,
   one-page, and two-page
   modes

▼ Use the right mouse
   button for fun and
   profit

▼ Learn a shortcut for
   typing words and
   phrases you use often

I HATE WORDPERFECT FOR WINDOWS!

This chapter does not contain a single thing you *have* to know to use WordPerfect. You could skip this chapter and still do what you need to do in WordPerfect.

But....

There's always a but. This chapter, more than any other, will help you use WordPerfect faster and—in many cases—easier. You'll learn how to accomplish with a couple of mouse clicks what would normally require wandering through several menus and dialog boxes. You'll learn how to make WordPerfect type words, phrases, and paragraphs by just pressing a few buttons. You'll even learn about that mysterious right button on your mouse.

Power Ties, Power Lunches, Power Bar

Using WordPerfect can be reminiscent of a scavenger hunt. You want to use one simple little feature, but finding that feature seems impossible. You might want to turn on double spacing, but find yourself wandering through a dark maze of menus, submenus, and dialog boxes before you finally find "Line Spacing" hidden in a dank, musty corner.

The Power Bar makes it so you don't have to go digging through WordPerfect to find the features you use most often. Instead, you just click a button at the top of the screen, and WordPerfect goes into action. No fiddling with dialog boxes and menus and red tape.

TIP

Whenever you can do something faster by using the Power Bar, this book points it out. Just look for a Power Bar button in the margin; this button tells you that you can simply click on a button rather than wade through lengthy steps.

The WordPerfect for Windows Power Bar.

Turning on the Power Bar (Where's that light switch?)

Take a good hard look at the top of the WordPerfect screen. Is the Power Bar there? (The last section showed a picture of the Power Bar.) If it is, move along to the next section—pass Go, collect $200. You don't need to read this section because the Power Bar is already turned on.

If, on the other hand, someone has turned off the Power Bar, here's what you do: choose View, Power Bar. The Power Bar appears under the menu bar. You won't have to turn it on again—WordPerfect remembers that you want it on.

Using the Power Bar (More power to ya)

There's not too much to know about the Power Bar—you usually just click on a button to turn on a feature. However, a few buttons do act a little differently, and you should know some tricks to get the most out of this snazzy tool.

Things to know about the Power Bar

✔ If you look closely, you'll see that some buttons are thinner than others. To use these thin buttons, move the insertion point to where you want the feature to do its thing, and then click the left button on your mouse.

continues

Things to know about the Power Bar (continued)

✔ A menu pops up when you click the wider buttons. For example, clicking on the Font button brings up a list of fonts.

✔ Some of Power Bar menus act differently than others. When you click some, the menu stays up until you click an option. With other buttons—such as the Font, Justification, and Line Spacing buttons—you click and hold the mouse button, and then drag to the option you want. When the option you want is highlighted, let go of the mouse button.

✔ If you click a button that brings up a menu, and then decide you don't want to use it, click somewhere outside the menu to make it disappear. Or, if it's the kind of menu that only stays up while you're holding down the mouse button, just let go of the mouse button without selecting an option.

✔ When your mouse pointer is over a button, the top of the WordPerfect window gives a brief description of what the button does. This description helps when the picture doesn't make sense.

✔ If a button is "dim" or "gray," you can't use the button right now. For example, the Cut and Copy buttons can't be used unless you've got something selected.

✔ If a button looks like it's pushed in, the feature's already on. For example, if the Bold button looks pushed in, the text at your insertion point is already bold. When this happens, you can turn the feature *off* by clicking its Power Bar button.

Which Buttons Do What?

To fit a lot of buttons in a little space, WordPerfect uses little pictures instead of words to describe the buttons. Unfortunately, we're not ancient Egyptians, so it's not easy to tell what those buttons do—at least not right off the bat. (As you use the buttons, you'll get used to some of them, and they won't seem so strange.)

Here's a quick rundown on what each button does, and where to look for more information on how the feature works.

Table 8.1 Power Bar Mysteries Revealed

Button	Name	What the Button Does
	New	Brings up a fresh, unused document window for you to work on. This doesn't close the other documents you've been using—just gives you another one—just so long as you don't have more than nine open at once. Chapter 10 talks about opening new documents.
	Open	The Open File dialog box appears, letting you select an existing document to work on. Learn about opening documents in Chapter 2.
	Save	Lets you name the document, if it doesn't have a name. Updates the document with your changes if you've already named it. See Chapter 1 to learn about saving.

continues

Table 8.1 Continued

Button	Name	What the Button Does
	Print	Displays the Print dialog box, where you can choose to print the whole document, just a page, or anywhere in between. See Chapter 4 for the details on printing.
	Cut	Removes the selected text and puts it in the computer's memory, so you can put (paste) the text somewhere else. See Chapter 2.
	Copy	Makes a copy of the selected text in the computer's memory, but also leaves the text in the document. The text can be "pasted" elsewhere. See Chapter 2.
	Paste	Puts text that has been cut or copied into the document at the insertion point. See Chapter 2 for the lowdown on pasting.
	Undo	Reverses the last thing you did, whether it was typing something you don't want, erasing something you do want, or accidentally putting formatting in a bad place. A *very* handy feature. Undo is covered in Chapter 2.

Button	Name	What the Button Does
FFF	Font	Causes a menu to pop down; this menu contains a list of fonts. Scroll through the menu until you see the font you need, and then click on it. Fonts are explained in Chapter 3.
‡A	Font Size	Displays a list of numbers—the sizes you can choose for your font. Scroll through the list, and then click the size you want. Font sizes are explained in Chapter 3.
B	Bold	Turns bold on. Or, if bold is already on, turns bold off. Check out Chapter 3 for the whole story.
I	Italic	Turns italic on. If italic is already on, turns it off. See Chapter 3.
U	Underline	Turns underline on. If underlining is already on, turns it off. See Chapter 3.
►L	Tab Set Menu	Lets you create a different tab set in your document. See Chapter 13 for details on using this button.
▦	Table Maker	Click and hold on this button, and then drag your mouse pointer to the dimensions of the table you want. Learn more about tables—and using this button—in Chapter 18.

continues

Table 8.1 Continued

Button	Name	What the Button Does
	Columns	Click and hold on this button, and then drag to the number of columns you want. When the correct number is selected, release the mouse button to turn on columns. Columns are explained in Chapter 17.
	Justification	Click and hold on this button, and then drag to how you want your text to line up with the margins. The little drawings give you an idea of each type of justification. Chapter 3 talks about justifying your text.
	Line Spacing	Click and hold on this button, and then drag to the line spacing you want. If none of the listed options suits your fancy, select the Other option to bring up the Line Spacing dialog box. You can set custom line spacing there. You can also double-click this button to bring up the Line Spacing dialog box. Learn more about line spacing in Chapter 3.
	Zoom	Click and hold on this button, and then drag to the Zoom setting you want. (*Zoom* is how big the text appears on-screen.) You can also double-click this button to bring up the Zoom dialog box. Learn about

Button	Name	What the Button Does
		Zoom in Chapter 10, if you must. (I personally try to stay away from features that sound like breakfast cereal.)
	Spell Check	Starts checking your document's spelling. Learn about spell-checking in Chapter 6.
	Thesaurus	Looks for synonyms and antonyms of a word. See Chapter 6 for more details.
	Grammar Checker	Checks your document's grammar. For the lowdown, see Chapter 6.
	Full Page Zoom	Gives you a quick preview of how your page will look when it's printed. This feature is covered in Chapter 4.
	Button Bar	Turns the Button Bar on or off. The Button Bar and the Power Bar are two different features; the Button Bar is discussed in the next section of this chapter.

Belly Up to the (Button) Bar

The Button Bar is the Power Bar's ugly cousin. It works in pretty much the same way, but because it shows both a picture of what the button does *and* a word-long description of what the button does, not quite as many buttons show. Plus, the buttons on the Button Bar are generally not as useful as the ones on the Power Bar.

Before you think that the Button Bar isn't worth your time, however, let me tell you about a few of its cool advantages. The Button Bar is easy to customize—you can very easily fill the Button Bar with the features that *you* use most often. And if that's not enough, you can move the Button Bar around—it can go on the top, bottom, left, or right side of the screen.

Using the Button Bar

To use the Button Bar, just click on the button that you want. The feature associated with that button jumps into action. If you click on the Indent button, for example, WordPerfect indents from the insertion point. If you click on the Date Text button, the current date is inserted in your document. And so on and so forth.

Checklist

✔ Not all the buttons on the Button Bar are very useful—some are strictly for computer guru types. The next section in this chapter, "Customizing the Button Bar," shows you how to display only the buttons you need on the Button Bar.

✔ The Button Bar is off limits when dialog boxes are showing. If you try to click on a Button Bar button when a dialog box is displayed, the computer chirps.

Customizing the Button Bar

The *idea* behind the Button Bar is great, but the Button Bar itself might not suit your fancy in its current style. But WordPerfect Corporation thought of everything—you can customize the Button Bar so that it's more to your liking. For instance, you may not like where the Button Bar appears. Under the menus is no good—it's too easy to hit a button when you want to pull down a menu and vice versa. Or you might not like the pictures shown on the buttons. Perhaps you would prefer just words. And what about those buttons you never use? Are you stuck with them? No. You can change the Button Bar to your liking.

Move It!

You've only got a certain amount of space on-screen, and having some of that space for typing would be nice. By getting rid of the pictures on the Button Bar and moving it so that it runs down the left side of the screen, you can fit more buttons into a smaller space. And because the Button Bar is no longer right under the menu bar, you won't have to hassle with accidentally pulling down menus when you want to click a button.

Here's how to take the pictures off the Button Bar and move the Button Bar to the left side of the screen:

1. Choose **File, Preferences.**

The Preferences dialog box appears. It's full of all kinds of funky icons. You're looking for the far left icon—the one that says *Button Bar*—in the second row.

2. Double-click on the **Button Bar** icon in the Preferences dialog box.

The Button Bar Preferences dialog box appears.

TIP

You can skip the first two steps in this process by moving the mouse pointer somewhere in the Button Bar that doesn't contain a button. When the mouse pointer changes to the shape of a hand, click the right mouse button. A menu pops out beside your mouse pointer. Choose the **P**references option.

3. Choose the Options button.

Now you're in the Button Bar Setup dialog box.

4. Choose **L**eft so that the Button Bar will go down the left side of the screen instead of across the top.

TIP

You might also want to experiment with putting the Button Bar on the bottom or right side of the screen. Or you may even want to put it back at the top. In step 2, just choose **B**ottom, **R**ight, or **T**op instead of **L**eft Side.

5. Choose **T**ext.

The pictures won't be part of the button anymore.

6. Choose OK, and then choose Close in the Button Bar Preferences dialog box.

The Button Bar is now on the left side of the screen. Notice that all the buttons fit on-screen with room to spare, and you have more typing space in your document window.

If you have the Button Bar go down the side of your screen, you'll have more room for additional buttons.

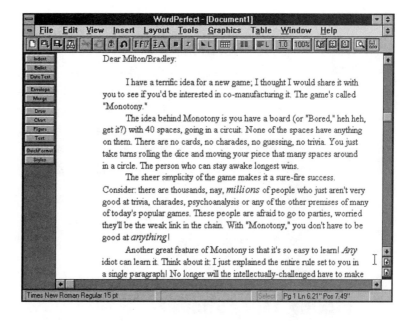

"I HATE THIS!"

Now these *&$@!? buttons are too small!

The Text Only buttons aren't for everybody. If you like the buttons to have the little pictures, follow the same steps. However, in step 4, choose either Top or Bottom. If the buttons have pictures on them, not many will fit down the side of the screen. Then, in step 5, choose Picture and Text, and choose OK.

TIP

There's a faster way you can move the Button Bar anywhere on the screen. Move the mouse pointer so that it's somewhere in the Button Bar, but not over a button. When the mouse pointer changes to a hand shape, press and hold the left mouse button, and drag the Button Bar to a new position. As you drag, an outline shape of the Button Bar moves with the mouse pointer; when you release the mouse button, the Button Bar appears in its new position.

You can drag the Button Bar to anywhere you want it—top, bottom, left, right, or anywhere in the middle.

Picking Your Buttons

You don't have to stick with the buttons that come on the WordPerfect Button Bar. You can add buttons for features you use a lot, and remove those buttons you rarely use.

The first step in changing which buttons you have on the Button Bar is to bring up the Edit Button Bar dialog box. Choose **File**, **Preferences**, double-click the Button Bar icon in the Preferences dialog box, and then choose **Edit**.

The Button Bar Editor dialog box appears. You need to move this dialog box a little in order to work with it. Click and hold on the top of the dialog box (where it reads *Button Bar Editor - WordPerfect*), and drag down just a little—maybe one-half inch or so. Let go of the mouse button; you should be able to see the menu bar now.

From here, it's easy to get rid of buttons you don't need and add ones you do.

✔ To get rid of a button you don't use, click on the button and drag it off the Button Bar. When you release the mouse button, the unwanted button disappears.

✔ When you've cleared out the buttons you *don't* need, you should have plenty of room on the Button Bar for buttons you *do* need. To add buttons, make sure that you're in the Button Bar Editor dialog box (choose **F**ile, **P**references, double-click the Button Bar icon in the Preferences dialog box, and then choose **E**dit). Then choose options from the menu bar as if you were going to use that feature. When you choose a feature, the button is added to the Button Bar.

✔ You also can move buttons around on the Button Bar. Just click on the button you want to move and drag it to a new location. When you let go of the mouse button, the button is moved. Any surrounding buttons move to make way for the new button.

✔ You can also add spaces to go between the buttons and to help group them. Notice the Spacers group box at the bottom of the Button Bar Editor dialog box. Click on the icon in that group box, and then drag the icon to where you want the spacer in the Button Bar. When you let go, WordPerfect inserts a space.

✔ You might have trouble dropping a button or space in exactly the right spot. If the button or space doesn't go where you want it, click and drag it again. You'll get the hang of it.

✔ When you're finished customizing the Button Bar, choose OK in the Button Bar Editor dialog box, choose **C**lose in the Button Bar Preferences dialog box, and then choose **C**lose in the Preferences dialog box.

CAUTION

It's tempting to put every feature under the sun on your Button Bar. *Don't!* If you get too many buttons on the Button Bar, little scroll bars appear at one side of the Button Bar. Then you have to scroll around looking for the desired button, which often takes more time than just going to it the old-fashioned way. A good rule of thumb is not to have more than 16 buttons on your Button Bar—and that's if you have the Button Bar going down one side of the screen with no pictures. If your Button Bar has pictures or goes across the top or bottom of the screen, you should have even fewer buttons.

"I HATE THIS!"

There's too much junk on my screen!

By the time you put a menu bar, a Power Bar, a Button Bar, scroll bars, and a status bar on your screen, it probably looks like you have a postage-stamp-sized area left to do your actual writing. You can use a trick to give yourself plenty of space for writing, and still have all your screen tools available. It's called *Hide Bars*.

When you use the Hide Bars feature, all those things on your screen disappear, leaving you with enough space to do your writing.

To turn on Hide Bars, choose **V**iew, **H**ide Bars. A dialog box comes up, telling you that all your editing bars are about to disappear. Choose OK.

When you want to bring your bars back, just press the Esc button, which should be at the top left side of your keyboard.

EXPERTS ONLY

Dr. Jekyll and Mr. Hide

If you find yourself using the Hide Bars feature a lot, you can set up WordPerfect so that it doesn't bring up that dialog box every time you turn on the feature. Choose **V**iew, **H**ide Bars as you usually do, but before you choose OK to turn on Hide Bars, choose the check box labeled **D**isable this message permanently. Now when you use this feature, WordPerfect assumes you know what you're doing and won't show the Hide Bars Information dialog box.

How Much Room for Your View?

How much can you stand to see on-screen at once? Do you want to see your margins, headers, footers, and page numbers along with your text? Or would you rather not think about those while you write? Maybe you're such a control freak that you want to see *two* pages at once.

However much you want to see while you work, WordPerfect can likely accommodate. You just need to know which option to choose from the View menu.

Choose your view

✔ *Draft Mode* is the simplest, cleanest view option. When you are using the Draft Mode, you don't see the headers, footers, margins, and page numbers on-screen—you just see the text you're writing. Choose **V**iew, **D**raft to turn on this mode. WordPerfect will give you the maximum possible space for your writing, not cluttering things up with the page elements you don't need to see while you're writing.

continues

135

✔ *Page Mode* shows you your margins, headers, footers—everything. This is a good mode to work in when you need to see how everything looks together. Choose **View**, **Page** to turn on Page Mode.

✔ *Two Page Mode* shows you two complete pages at a time. The problem is, the text is so dinky that you can't tell what it says. This mode is best for just checking to see that the general "look" of the document is right.

✔ Click the Full Page Zoom button on the Power Bar. You'll be able to see the whole page, and you should still be able to read the text—but just barely.

The Magical Right Mouse Button

For years, computer users have wondered about the right mouse button. It's a mystery rivaled only by how the pyramids were built, or how *Dukes of Hazzard* stayed on the air for so long.

Wonder no more. WordPerfect makes the right mouse button a useful tool. If you remember to use the right mouse button when you're editing in WordPerfect, you'll find it saves all kinds of time.

The general idea behind the right mouse button is this: when you click it, a menu pops up beside the mouse pointer, and you can choose one of the options from that menu. Just choose the option you want by clicking on it—with either your left or right mouse button. What's on the menu? It depends on where your mouse is when you clicked.

For example, if you have selected text and you click the right mouse button, a menu comes up with Cut, Copy, Paste, Delete, Font, Quick Format, and Speller. These are all features you might want to use when you have text selected.

For another example, say you click the right mouse button when the mouse pointer is positioned over a scroll bar. A menu with Go To, Bookmarks, and Preferences comes up. In this case, the Bookmarks and Preferences options are pretty much for computer-guru types, but the Go To option is great for jumping to a certain page. Click on this option for the Go To dialog box, type the number of the page you want to move to in the Page **N**umber text box, and then choose OK.

The following checklist tells you some other things you can do with the right mouse button.

Right mouse magic

✔ If your mouse pointer is in a document window without text selected, the right mouse button brings up a menu with Paste, Font, Quick Format, Speller, Center, Flush Right, and Indent. The right mouse button is often the quickest way to get to each of these features.

✔ Clicking the right mouse button when your pointer is over the Button Bar brings up a menu containing Edit, Preferences, and Hide Button Bar, as well as a list of other Button Bars you might want to try.

✔ Clicking over the status bar brings up the Hide Status Bar and Preferences menu. You can choose Hide Status Bar to give yourself more space to work in, but you probably won't ever want to mess with the Status Bar Preferences. (To bring the status bar back onto the screen, choose **V**iew, **S**tatus Bar.)

✔ You can click the right button over the Power Bar to get a **P**references and **H**ide Power Bar menu. Don't mess with the **P**references option, but you might occasionally want to hide the Power Bar to give yourself extra room to work. When you want to bring back the Power Bar, choose **V**iew, **P**ower Bar.

CAUTION

A lot of the options in the menus that appear when you click the right mouse button are really meant for guru types. If you don't recognize an option in the menu, you'll be better off not trying it.

If you really, really must try it because you're so curious you could burst, make sure that you save your document first. Then if you wreck your new document, you can close it without saving and still have your last saved version.

Go, Speed Writer, Go! (Using abbreviations)

How many times do you think I've used the word "WordPerfect" in this book? Probably just over a million. How many times have I *typed* "WordPerfect"? Once. I've been using the Abbreviation feature, which lets you create shortcuts for words, phrases, paragraphs—you name it—that you use frequently. Instead of having to type out the whole thing, you just press a couple of key letters, and then tell WordPerfect to expand it into the full text you want.

If you want to use Abbreviations to cut down on repetitive typing, follow these steps:

1. Select the text you want a shortcut for.

For example, I selected the word *WordPerfect*, since I wanted a shortcut for typing this word. You can select much more text than that—anything you use frequently.

2. Choose Insert, Abbreviations.

The Abbreviations dialog box comes up. The list box shows any abbreviations you've created previously. The first time you see this dialog box, the list box will be empty.

3. Choose **Create**.

The Create Abbreviation dialog box comes up. Here's where you decide what the shortcut letters are for the text you've selected.

4. Type a few letters that will remind you of the text you've selected.

For example, since I made a shortcut for *WordPerfect*, I typed **WP** here. If you had selected *National Aeronautics Space Administration*, you might type **NASA** here. If you had selected your mother's address, you might type **Mom** here.

5. Choose **OK**.

6. Choose **Close**.

Your abbreviation is ready.

Using your abbreviations

✔ Once you've created an abbreviation, you can use it any time you want the text in your document. Type the abbreviation—the few letters—for your text, and then press Ctrl+A. Your "abbreviated" version of the text disappears, replaced by the full version.

✔ If you forget the abbreviation for certain text, choose Insert, Abbreviations. The list box in the Abbreviations dialog box contains a list of all the abbreviations you've created. When you select an abbreviation in the list box, the bottom of the dialog box shows the beginning of what text that abbreviation stands for. Choose Close to leave the dialog box.

continues

CHAPTER 8

Using your abbreviations (continued)

✔ If you forget to press Ctrl+A after typing the åbbreviation for certain text, you can expand it later. Just move the insertion point so that it's anywhere in the abbreviation, and then press Ctrl+A. The larger text will appear.

✔ Your abbreviations will be available to you now and forever. You can use them in any document, any time you use WordPerfect.

PART III

Files and Documents

Includes:

CHAPTER 9

Working with Files
(WordPerfect's Answer to the Overstuffed Filing Cabinet)

IN A NUTSHELL

- ▼ Decipher DOS path names
- ▼ View a document before retrieving it
- ▼ Open a file for editing
- ▼ Find files
- ▼ Print documents from the Open File dialog box
- ▼ Delete files you no longer need
- ▼ Create directories
- ▼ Change directories
- ▼ Copy files
- ▼ Move files from one directory to another

When you work with WordPerfect, you've got to learn some things about managing files. *Files* are the documents you've named and put on your hard disk (and floppy disks, too). They're sitting on your hard disk right now, seemingly multiplying at a furious rate. To keep your files from getting out of control, you're going to have to pay a little attention to them.

To begin, you need a small dose of DOS—even though you're working in Windows. This chapter starts by explaining *paths* and *directories*, as they relate to files. You probably should read this section.

Then this chapter covers what you can do to a file: open it, print it, delete it, curl it, clip it, brush it, snip it. Skim the headings to find procedures that interest you. File management isn't a daily task, but it is something you should know how to do.

Files, Directories, and Paths! Oh My!

Files are the individual documents that you store on a disk. Rather than lump all files in one pile on the hard disk, you can—and should—divide the hard disk into sections. These sections are called *directories*.

One main directory, called the *root directory*, houses all the other directories. You can have many directories within the root directory. You can also have directories within directories within directories. (Sometimes the term *subdirectory* rather than *directory* is used; a subdirectory is a directory that is kept in another directory. The two terms mean the same thing.)

BUZZWORDS

DIRECTORY

A directory is a section of your hard disk. If your hard disk is an entire house, a directory is one room. The path tells you how to get to that room: go through the dining room to get to the kitchen.

The route through all the directories is called the *path*. For instance, decode this path:

```
C:\WPWIN60\WPDOCS\RECIPES\COOKIE.WPD
```

✔ C: indicates the drive (in this case, drive C).

✔ \ (backslash) is the name of the root directory.

✔ WPWIN60 is the first directory.

✔ WPDOCS is in the WPWIN60 directory.

✔ RECIPES is a directory within WPDOCS.

✔ COOKIE.WPD is the file name.

Why is all this information important? When you start to organize your files into directories and you can't find a file that you're sure you saved, you'll need some clues to decode the path and the directory structure.

The Amazing Open File Dialog Box (Open Sesame)

If you've ever opened a document you've saved before, you're familiar with the basics of the Open File dialog box. What you may not know is that you can do just about all your file management from this one little dialog box.

The Open File dialog box helps you manage your files. You see a list of files; then you can select the appropriate file and open it, print it, copy it, or delete it—whatever you want.

To bring up the Open File dialog box, choose **File, Open**—or, if you like, you can click on the Power Bar's Open File button.

TIP

If you like to keep your hands on the keyboard, you can bring up the Open File dialog box by pressing Ctrl+O.

The Open File dialog box comes up.

I HATE WORDPERFECT FOR WINDOWS!

The directory you're looking at

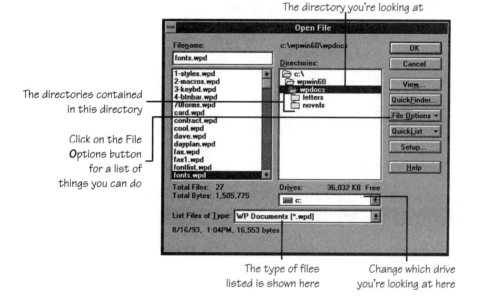

The directories contained in this directory

Click on the File Options button for a list of things you can do

The type of files listed is shown here

Change which drive you're looking at here

Open File facts

✔ Files are sorted alphabetically.

✔ To open a file, just double-click the file name.

✔ By default, WordPerfect shows only files with a WPD extension. That's because WordPerfect automatically gives your file names this WPD extension whenever you save a file without typing an extension of your own.

continues

✔ If you want the Open File dialog box to show all files, click the down-arrow button in the List Files of **T**ype box. Then scroll up to the top of the list, where it says "All Files." Click this option, and all files—not just ones that end in WPD—are shown.

✔ To look at the files on a different drive (such as drive A or B), click the down-arrow button in the Drives box. A menu containing all the drives you have available pops up. From this menu, click the drive you want to look at.

✔ To find the file you want to work with, scroll through the Filename list box. Or click in the list box and begin typing the name of the file; WordPerfect will begin searching for it. If you're certain of the file name, just type it in the text box above the Filename list box.

✔ Your current path is shown as a series of "open" folders in the **D**irectories list box. Directories within the directory you're currently working on are shown as closed folders. To look at the files in a different directory, just double-click that folder.

✔ To see a different path, go back to the root directory by double-clicking it and then double-clicking the successive directories that belong in the path. For example, if you're in the C:\WPDOCS directory but want to go to the C:\WINDOWS directory, double-click the C:\ folder; then double-click the WINDOWS folder.

✔ When you want to leave the Open File dialog box without actually opening a document, choose Cancel.

✔ You may see dialog boxes similar to the Open File dialog box elsewhere in WordPerfect, like when you want to open a graphic. These boxes *work* the same way, too, so you don't have to figure out a whole new set of rules for using those dialog boxes.

Previewing a Document
(The Peeping Tom feature)

You've gotten to the Open File dialog box. You've got a document high-lighted. You even think it's the one you want to work on—but you're not sure. If only you could take a look at the file... with WordPerfect, you can.

To peek at the file (that is, to use the View feature), simply highlight the file in the Open File dialog box and choose the View button.

Checklist

✔ When you're finished looking at the document, choose OK to open the document, click another file name you want to view, or double-click the control box in the upper left corner of the View box to close the View feature.

✔ If the first screen of the document isn't enough to tell whether you've got the correct file, use the scroll bars to see more of the text. You can continue this process through the whole document, if that's the kind of thing you enjoy.

✔ You can't edit the document in the View box.

✔ The View feature is good, but it's not exact. It can't display things like fonts and tables.

✔ You can use all the buttons and options in the Open File dialog box while the View window is showing. So, you can change direc-tories, select new files, or even choose Cancel to leave the View window and the Open File dialog box.

EXPERTS ONLY

The document combo platter

Once in a while, you might want to insert one document into another document. Begin by opening the first document. Move the insertion point to where you want to insert the second document. Choose Insert, File. Then select the document that you want to insert, and choose Insert. A box appears, asking whether you want to insert the selected file into the current document. Choose Yes. The second document is plopped right into the first document, beginning at the insertion point. You then save the combined document with a new name.

What's Its Name?

When you haven't used a file in a while, you may forget its name. It's often easier to remember certain words you used in the document than to remember the actual name of the document. Fortunately for you, WordPerfect can search through your files for text that you specify, and then tell you what files contain the text.

To look for files that contain certain words, you need to be in the Open File dialog box. Then follow these steps:

1. Choose QuickFinder.

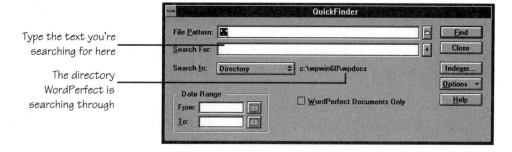

Type the text you're searching for here

The directory WordPerfect is searching through

2. Click in the Search For text box, type the word that you want WordPerfect to look for; then choose OK.

Actually, you can type more than one word if you like, but most people get best results when they stick to just one word. Use a word that you're sure has something to do with the file you're using. For instance, if you've just written a Master's thesis on armadillo farms, the word *armadillo* is a safe bet.

WordPerfect spins its wheels for a minute, scanning through all your files for the text you need, and then shows the Search Results dialog box. Only the files containing the word you specified are in the list. You should be able to find the file you want from this narrowed list. Select the file; then choose Open (or use any of the other options available in the Open File dialog box).

Checklist

✔ If you're still not sure which file is the one you're looking for, highlight one you *think* is right and use the View feature. (The section "Preview a Document" earlier in this chapter explains the View feature.) Preview the files in the list until you find the one you need.

continues

I HATE WORDPERFECT FOR WINDOWS!

✔ If you've got a lot of documents in the directory, WordPerfect might need several minutes to search all the files. Give yourself plenty of time when you start this process.

✔ If none of the files contain the word you typed, a box appears telling you No Files Found. Choose OK to go back to the QuickFinder dialog box; then try one of the following methods in this list to find the file.

✔ From the QuickFinder dialog box, click and hold on the Search In pop-up menu. Choose Subtree from the menu that appears. Word-Perfect will search through this directory and any directories contained in this directory. Choose Find to begin searching.

✔ Click and hold on the Search In pop-up menu. Choose Disk from the menu. If the drive shown to the right of this pop-up menu isn't the one you want to search, click on the drive; this brings up a pop-up menu showing the available drives. Click the drive you want to search through. Choose Find again, but expect to wait for a while—WordPerfect is going to look through the whole drive.

Selecting Lots of Files

Normally, when you use list boxes in WordPerfect, you select just one item. In the Open File dialog box, though, you can select several files at once. Why on earth would you want to do that? The Open File dialog box lets you do certain things with the selected file—or files.

For example, if you have one file selected, you open that one file; but if you have four files selected, you can open all four files in one fell swoop.

(How to work with more than one document at once is covered in Chapter 10.) In the same way, you can print more than one file at once, delete several files at a time, copy lots of files, and so on.

Here are some techniques for selecting more than one file in the Open File dialog box:

Selected selections on selecting files

✔ To select several files in a row, click on the first file you want selected, and then drag down to the last file you want selected.

✔ To select files that aren't all together, hold down your Ctrl key while you click individual files.

✔ If you want to select a series of files, skip some, then select another series, click and drag for the first series, move your mouse pointer to where the second series should begin, then hold down the Ctrl key while you click and drag for the second series of files.

✔ If you decide you don't want a file selected after all, hold down the Ctrl key while you click the selected file to deselect it.

✔ If you want to deselect all the selected files, just click a different file. The file you click will be selected; all others will be deselected.

✔ You can select files using your arrow keys, too. Press Shift+arrow key to select series of files.

✔ A tricky way to select a series of files is to click the first file you want selected, move your mouse pointer to the last file you want selected, hold down the Shift key, and then click.

✔ Once you've selected the files you want, you're ready to open, copy, delete, or print them (or whatever else you want), pretty much as if they were all just a single file.

I HATE WORDPERFECT FOR WINDOWS!

Printing Documents from the Open File Dialog Box (Avoid the middleman)

When it comes right down to it, the main reason you use WordPerfect is to get your words onto paper. The File Manager lets you print your documents without having to go through the hassle of opening them first.

To print documents from the File Manager, first make sure that your printer is on and set to print. Then follow these steps:

1. Highlight the file or files you want to print.

2. Choose the File Options button, and then choose **Print** from the menu.

CAUTION

> Make sure you choose **Print**—not Print **List**! They're close together and look a lot alike; it's easy to confuse the two. The only time you should choose Print **List** is if you want to print a list of your file names.

Another dialog box appears, asking you whether you want to print the file or files.

3. Choose **Print**.

Your printer begins grinding away.

EXPERTS ONLY

For File Manager gurus only

Windows comes with a program designed specifically for doing everything the rest of this chapter talks about. If you already know how to use File Manager, there's no reason for you to read the rest of this chapter. The File Manager program can handle all your file management needs just as well (and better, in many cases) as WordPerfect.

Deleting Files

Murphy's Law: The minute after you delete a file, you'll need it. Granted, you *do* want to erase files from time to time; it keeps your hard disk from getting cluttered and gaining unsightly pounds. But be careful! If you even *suspect* that you might need a document sometime in the future, don't erase it.

Now that you're too scared to ever delete anything, here are the steps to erase documents you no longer need:

1. Bring up the Open File dialog box and highlight the file or files to delete.

2. Choose File Options, Delete.

   A dialog box appears, asking whether you want to delete the file (or files).

3. Choose Delete.

Creating a New Directory

Few things in life make you feel so organized and purposeful as when you create a new directory for a certain type of document. After all, out of the chaos of the hard disk, you've made an organized home for a specific type of file such as letters or memos.

The nice thing about creating new directories in WordPerfect is that it's easy. Bring up the Open File dialog box; then just follow these steps:

1. Choose File Options, Create Directory.

The Create Directory dialog box appears, asking you to type a new directory.

2. Type the name of the directory that you want to create.

The directory name you type will be put inside the directory beside Current Directory. For example, if C:\WPWIN60\WPDOCS is beside Current Directory and you type **LETTERS**, you'll have created a C:\WPWIN60\WPDOCS\LETTERS directory. If you want to create the directory in a different path, type the full path name, such as **C:\LETTERS\PERSONAL**.

3. Choose Create.

Now you're back at the Open File dialog box. Your directory has been created.

✔ WordPerfect will do whatever is necessary to create your new directory. If you're in the Create Directory dialog box and type **C:\DREAMS\STRANGE**, WordPerfect will create the directory, even if it has to create the DREAMS directory and then create the STRANGE directory to put in it.

✔ Directory names follow the same rules as file names: they should have eight or fewer characters and use only letters and numbers.

Copying Files (The file photocopier)

In this wondrous computer age, people trade computer files like they used to trade baseball cards. Here's how you copy files:

1. Bring up the File Open dialog box.

2. Move to the directory that has the files you want to copy.

3. Highlight the file or files you want to copy.

4. Choose File Options, **C**opy.

The Copy File dialog box appears.

5. Type the path where you want a copy of the files; then choose Copy.

For example, you might type **C:\WPDOCS\POEMS**.

The file is copied to the directory you specified.

✔ Ordinarily, WordPerfect won't copy a file into the new directory if there's already a file with the same name. If you want WordPerfect to copy your files even if there's already a file with the same name, uncheck the **Don't replace files with the same size, date, and time** check box in the Copy File dialog box. Now, if there is a file with the same name, WordPerfect will bring up a dialog box, asking whether to overwrite the old file. Choose **Yes** if you want to replace the file already in the directory with the one you've selected and are copying.

✔ When you type the path you want to copy the file to, you can also type a different file name at the end of the path. The file is copied to the new directory, but it has the new name you specify.

✔ If you don't feel like typing the path name to copy the files to, click the Folder button beside the Copy Selected Files To text box. This brings up the Select Directory dialog box in which you can browse through directories until you've found the one you want. Choose OK, and then choose **C**opy to copy the files into that directory.

Moving Files

When you're ready to roll up your sleeves and do some serious hard disk housecleaning, the File Manager's Move feature can be a big help. It moves files from one place to another. For instance, you might want to move all the chapters of your Great American Novel into their own directory. Here's how you do it:

1. Bring up the Open File dialog box.

2. Move to the directory that has the files you want to move.

3. Highlight the file or files you want to move.

4. Choose File Options, Move.

WordPerfect brings up the Move File dialog box.

5. Type the path you want the file to go to, such as **C:\WPWIN60\WPDOCS\LETTERS**. Then choose **Move**.

Your files are moved from the old directory to the new one. No U-Haul trucks or burly professional movers required.

Checklist

✔ If you're moving just one file, you can type a different file name after the path name, such as

C:\WPWIN60\WPDOCS\LETTERS\NEWNAME.WPD.

This moves and renames the document.

✔ If you just want to change the document's name, type a new file name. Don't type a path. WordPerfect renames the file and leaves it in the current directory.

✔ You can use the file folder button to the right of the text box to find the directory you want to move your file or files to. Click the button to bring up the Select Directory dialog box. Double-click the directories and subdirectories until you've found the path you want; then choose OK. This takes you back to the Move Files dialog box, where you should choose **M**ove.

CHAPTER 10

Working with Lots of Documents

IN A NUTSHELL

- ▼ Use more than one document at once
- ▼ Move from document to document
- ▼ Tile your document windows
- ▼ Cascade your document windows
- ▼ Get a close-up (or far-away view) of your document with Zoom

With WordPerfect, you can work on up to nine documents at once. Who would want to write or edit nine documents at the same time? Sybil, maybe?

You probably won't ever need to work on nine documents at the same time, but there may come a time when you want to work on at least two or three documents at once. It's nice to be able to copy a paragraph from one document, switch over to another, and paste the paragraph. Or you might want to look at two documents at once, side-by-side. You can do it all in WordPerfect, and you learn how in this chapter.

Working with More than One Document (DocumentFest '94)

The ability to have more than one document available is a real productivity enhancer. You can type away on that memo for a few minutes, and then switch over and work on your quarterly report. When you need to, you can switch back to the memo and hammer away. (Never mind that you can also use this feature to work on that *National Enquirer* article about how your boss is really an Evil Alien from planet Yechh, and then quickly switch to that memo when your boss steps in.)

There are a couple of things you need to know about working on more than one document at a time. First, you need to know how to *get* more than one document going in WordPerfect; then you need to know how to switch between documents.

Starting a Fresh Document

You're typing away; everything's going just fine. Suddenly, a flash inspiration comes—and you want to type it before it slips away. You don't have to close the document you're working on; just start a new document.

To start a new document, just choose **File**, **New**. Or, if you like using the Power Bar, click on the New Document button.

TIP

If you want to start a new document without moving your hands from the keyboard, press Ctrl+N.

A blank document window appears, where you can begin typing and editing as you do in any document (and don't forget to save this new document, too). Don't worry, you haven't lost your other document; you can see how to switch back to it just a little later in this chapter.

You can use this technique to start as many new document windows as you want—as long as your total number of documents is no greater than nine.

Opening Existing Documents

If you want to work on a couple of files you've got saved on disk, WordPerfect lets you do that, too. Choose **File**, **Open** to see the Open File dialog box. Double-click the document you want to use, and it's opened into a new document window.

I HATE WORDPERFECT FOR WINDOWS!

✔ This doesn't mean that other document windows you've had open are automatically closed—they're still open. See the "Switching Documents" section coming up next to learn how to switch between document windows you have open.

✔ You can open more than one document at once. At the Open File dialog box, hold down the Ctrl button while you click each file you want to open. When you've got them all selected, choose OK. All the files (as long as the total doesn't come to more than nine) open, each into a separate document window.

Switching Documents (Changing channels)

Once you've got more than one document open, you'll want to switch between them. To do this, follow these steps:

1. Choose the Window menu.

The Window menu pops up. At the bottom of the menu is a list of all the documents you have open. If the documents have file names, they are shown.

Choose the file
name you want
to work in on the
Window menu

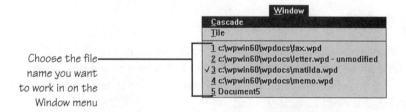

164

2. Choose the file you want to work on.

That document pops up, and you can get to work.

Checklist

✔ If something like Document6 is listed as one of the items in your Window menu, the document hasn't been named. You can still switch to it by choosing that option.

✔ When you pull down the **Window** menu, a check box appears by the document you are using right now. So there's no point in choosing that option.

✔ If you haven't changed a document since you last saved it, the word unmodified appears by the file name in the Window menu.

✔ If you have document windows set up so that two or more appear on-screen (you'll learn how to do that in "Seeing is Believing," the next section in this chapter), you don't have to use the Window menu to switch documents. Just click somewhere in the document you want to work on.

Seeing Is Believing (Seeing more than one document at once)

You've got a few documents running at the same time. Fine. But what if you want to compare them—to look at more than one document at once? Well, you can do that, too. You just need to know the mysteries of tiling and cascading. What do these mysterious terms mean? Read on to find out.

Tiling

You can tell WordPerfect to show each of your document windows on-screen by using the Tile command. When you do this, each of your document windows gets equal space on your screen. This is nice when you want to compare two documents or move information from one to another.

To "tile" your document windows, choose **Window**, **Tile**.

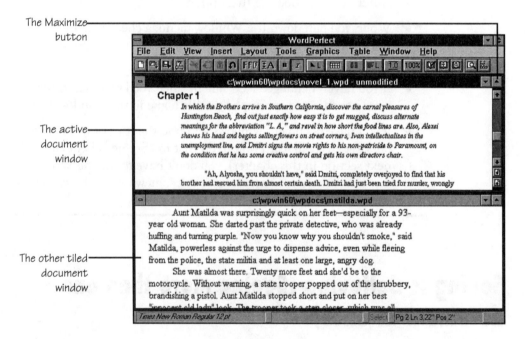

The Maximize button

The active document window

The other tiled document window

BUZZWORDS

ACTIVE DOCUMENT

When you have more than one document open at a time, you can only work on one of them at a time. The document you can work on is called the "active" document. You can tell which document window is active by looking to see which one has scroll bars and a different-color title bar.

Tile talk

✔ Click on the document window you want to make active. You can then work in it normally.

✔ If you use the Tile feature with more than two or three documents open, there won't be enough space on-screen to see *any* of the documents very well.

✔ You can cut or copy text from one tiled document and paste it into the other document, just the same as you would normally use cut, copy, and paste. This is one of the most useful things about tiled documents.

✔ When you're tired of working in tiny, tiled document windows, click one of the document window's Maximize buttons (in the upper right corner of the document window). The window fills up the whole screen. You can now switch back to the other window by choosing **Window**, and then choosing the option for the other document.

Cascading Windows

Another way you can see all your document windows at once is to use the Cascade command. When you *cascade* your windows, they appear one after another for sort of a waterfall effect, like this:

Click on the
document
window you
want to use

Cascaded
documents, piled
on top of each
other

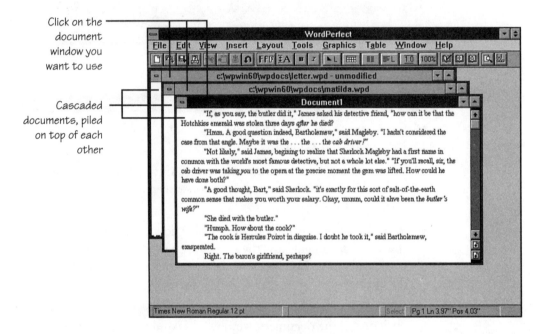

To get this funky look for your document windows, choose **Window, Cascade**.

Checklist

✔ Why would you want to use the cascade look for your windows? It shows the title bar to each of your document windows, so you can easily switch to any of them, plus there's enough space that you can see a respectable amount of text in the active document window.

✔ With your document windows cascaded, you can only see the title of each document (except the one on top). Click on the part of the

window you *can* see to bring the rest up forward, so you can work on it. You can click on different documents, looking for the one you want to edit.

✔ You may want to move a cascaded document window to a different part of the screen. To learn how to perform this neat trick, read the following Experts-Only sidebar later in this chapter (if you dare).

✔ Cascaded document windows are pretty tiny, so you'll probably want to have one of your documents fill the screen again before too long. To do this, click the document window's Maximize button.

EXPERTS ONLY

Movers and shakers

Here's a little bit of Windows magic: you can custom-size those document windows. You can also move them around on-screen. All you need to know is a few tricks, and how to use a few buttons.

First off, you can't move a document window when it's maximized. To make your document window so it isn't maximized, click the Restore button at the far right side of Word-Perfect's menu bar. (There will be two identical buttons on top of each other; click the lower one.) If your documents have been tiled or cascaded, they're already not maximized, so you don't have to click this button.

Now you can move or size the window. To size the window, move your mouse pointer to one of the corners of the document window. When the pointer turns into diagonal arrows, click and drag the window to be the new size you want.

You can move the window by clicking at the top of the window (where the document name is) and dragging to where you want the window.

Zoom!

Most of the time you're writing and editing in WordPerfect, you'll want the text to appear big enough for you to read, without being so big that you feel like you're looking at the screen through Mr. Magoo glasses. Every once in a while, though, you may want to get an extreme close-up of part of your document, or you may want to back away to get the big picture. The Zoom feature lets you do either of these.

"I HATE THIS!"

Using Two Page mode? Then forget Zoom

The Zoom feature can't be used when you're using WordPerfect's Two-Page View mode. Sorry. If you want to zoom in or out, you'll have to use the Draft or Page mode.

To take a close (or far away) look at your document text, choose **V**iew, **Z**oom to bring up the Zoom dialog box. Click the radio button beside the size at which you want to see your text; then choose OK.

Things you can do in the Zoom dialog box

✔ Each of the numbers in the Zoom dialog box is a percentage of your text's actual size. So 50% means your text will appear half as big as it will actually print. 200% means the text will appear twice as big as it will print.

✔ The Margin Width option is my personal favorite for day-to-day typing needs. It means that the text pretty much goes from the left to right side of your screen. This way, your text is just a touch bigger than if you see the margin white space—and bigger is better, for most people's eyes.

✔ Choose the Page **W**idth option when you need to see the margin white space as you type.

✔ Choose **F**ull Page when you want to see the whole page all at once. Unless you have a big monitor, this means the text will appear so small that you won't be able to read it.

✔ The best way to quickly see the whole page is to not use the Zoom feature at all. Instead, just click the Power Bar's Full Page Zoom button. You'll see your whole page. When you want to go back to a normal view of your document (so you can read the text), click the same button again.

TIP

If you use the Zoom feature a lot, you can use it faster by using the Zoom pop-up button on the Power Bar. Click and hold on the button to make the menu pop up. Then, still holding down the mouse button, drag your mouse until you highlight the zoom setting you want to use. Release the mouse button to turn that zoom setting on.

Bonus Zoom tip: If you want to go to the Zoom dialog box, just double-click the Zoom pop-up button.

PART IV

The Impressive Stuff

Includes:

CHAPTER 11

I Need To Do This NOW!

(Using WordPerfect Templates)

IN A NUTSHELL

- ▼ Meet the lifesaving Template feature
- ▼ Save your personal template info
- ▼ Make a memo, form a fax, and write a letter

Some types of documents require you to type the same thing over and over. Think about a memo. You've got the word *memo*, the *to*, the *from*, the *date*, and the *subject*. All the same words, typed over and over for each memo. Isn't there a better way?

Of course. Templates. You can use WordPerfect templates for the repetitive parts of documents. Then you just fill in the part that *does* change—the body of the letter or memo, the recipient's fax number, whatever.

This chapter shows you how to use WordPerfect's Template feature, and even how to create your own template for writing a letter.

Template Basics

No matter *which* template you decide to use, you use this method to turn on a template:

1. Choose **File, Template**. Or press Ctrl+T if you've got your hands firmly rooted to the keyboard.

The Templates dialog box appears, with a list of templates you can use.

2. Scroll through the list of templates until you see the one you want to use.

3. Double-click the template.

The template appears in a new document window.

The first time you use the Templates feature, a Personalize Your Templates dialog box appears, telling you that you need to type some information about yourself for the templates to use. Choose OK. Next, the Enter Your Personal Information dialog box comes

up, where you need to type your name, title, company name, address, telephone number, and fax number. This information will be used in various templates, like in memos and letterheads. Type your info, pressing Tab—not Enter—to move from one text box to the next. When you're done typing your personal information, choose OK.

"I HATE THIS!"

Whoops! I pressed Enter after typing one of the lines

Most people automatically press Enter after typing a line of text like their name or address, so don't feel bad if you do. When you press Enter before filling out all the text boxes in the Enter Your Personal Information dialog box, a message box appears, asking whether you want to go back and finish typing your personal information. Choose **Yes**, and then press Tab until you're at the next text box you need to fill out.

4. If the Template Information dialog box appears, fill out the text boxes, and then choose OK.

This dialog box contains information specific to the template you've chosen. For example, if you've chosen a Memo template, the dialog box will contain Name, CC, and Subject text boxes. After you type this information and choose OK, the information is automatically inserted—in the correct place—into your document.

5. Fill in the text that needs to go into the document.

Checklist

✔ Even though the document window opened by the template contains words before you begin working, the document doesn't have a name. Treat it as if it were a new document—name it and save it regularly.

continues

✔ When you choose a template to work on, you're just working on a *copy* of the template—you're not changing the real thing. This means that you can use the same template over and over.

✔ If you're not sure which template to use, scroll through the list of templates and highlight the one you *think* you want. A description of the template appears in the Description box below the list box. If that's not the right template, continue highlighting templates until you find the one you want. Once you've highlighted the right template, choose OK.

✔ If you need to change some of your personal information for the template feature—if your job title changes or you get a new phone number for instance—start a template normally. When the Template Information dialog box appears, choose the Personal Info button to go to the Enter Your Personal Information dialog box. From here, you can change your personal information in any of the text boxes; then choose OK.

✔ If the description of the template isn't enough to tell you whether you want to use it, highlight a template you're curious about and choose View. A preview of the template's contents appears beside the list of templates on-screen. With this preview screen showing, you can continue to click on templates you might want to use— the preview screen shows whichever template is highlighted. Once you've found the template you want, choose OK.

✔ Don't expect too much from the preview screen. It just shows the text—not all the fancy formatting—of the template.

✔ The next section in this chapter gives you the lowdown on some of the templates you might want to use.

These Are a Few of My Favorite Templates

WordPerfect comes with several templates. You'll find some of them useful. Others, you probably won't use at all. It all depends on the kind of work you do. The templates listed here are all pretty general-purpose, heavy-duty, everyday-workhorse kinds of templates that just about everybody can use. Try looking at others to see if they can help you in your work.

✔ **Certif1** and **Certif2**: Use these templates to give out "Certificates of Achievement" to your friends, family, and coworkers. Heck, you may as well make certificates for your enemies, too. You can give that sneaky, snivelly person down the hall a certificate of achievement for being the Brown-Noser of the Month. Imagine how pleased he'll be. Certif01 is a straightforward certificate; Certif02 is more flowery.

✔ **Fax1** and **Fax2**: These are generic fax cover sheets. Fax02 is a bigger, bolder, badder version, with the words "Fax Transmission" printed so large you should be able to read it from 100 yards (just in case the mood to do some long-distance fax reading strikes you).

✔ **Letter1- Letter5:** These are probably the most useful templates of all. Use them whenever you need to write a letter. These create various letterheads for you, prompt you for the mailing address and greeting, and even pre-type your signature block—all you have to do is type the main part of the letter.

✔ **Memo1-Memo3**: Use these templates to create snappy-looking memos. The Memo1 template gives your memo a less-formal look, while Memo2 makes your memo look all dressed up in a blue blazer and yellow power tie.

✔ **Newsltr1**: If you want a head start in making a fancy-looking three-column newsletter, this template can help. It asks you for the name of your newsletter, the issue number, and the date, so all you have to do is come up with clever article ideas to write.

CHAPTER 12

The Perfect Page

(Making Your Text Go Where You Want It to Go)

IN A NUTSHELL

- ▼ Change the margins
- ▼ Add page numbers
- ▼ Center your text between the top and bottom margins
- ▼ Create headers and footers
- ▼ Put a border around a page
- ▼ Put a border around a paragraph
- ▼ Use WordPerfect to make labels

This is the chapter that will make you glad you've decided to move from your typewriter to WordPerfect. The stuff in this chapter is incredibly difficult—and some of it's nearly impossible—to do with the ol' Remington.

You'll change your margins with the greatest of ease; you'll have Word-Perfect automatically number your pages. You'll find that centering text between top and bottom margins—like you do for cover pages—is no longer something to lose sleep over. You'll even find that truly fancy stuff—like headers, footers, borders, and labels—is easy to do with WordPerfect.

Adjusting Your Margins (Corral your text)

Margins are the white space that surrounds the text on a page. Word-Perfect sets up standard 1-inch margins all the way around the page. These settings work for most documents. If you need to tinker with the number of words on the page—cram more text or have less text—change the margins.

Here's how you set new margins:

1. Move the insertion point to where you want the new margins to begin.

New margin settings apply from the page and paragraph where the insertion point is currently positioned. The new margins apply from that point to the end of the document—or to the next place you change the margins. You usually want to be at the top of the document when you change margins so that the new settings apply to the entire document. To get to the beginning of the document, press Ctrl+Home.

TIP

When you set new top and bottom margins, they apply from the page your insertion point is positioned in right now. When you set new left and right margins, on the other hand, they apply from the current paragraph. So if you want your new left and right margins to apply from the beginning of the page, make sure that the insertion point is positioned at the beginning of the page when you begin these steps.

No matter what kind of margin you set, that margin applies to the bottom of the document, or to where you set a different margin.

2. Choose Layout, Margins.

Up comes the Margins dialog box.

3. Select the Left, Right, Top, or Bottom text box and type in a measurement. Do this for every margin you want to change. You can also click the up- and down-arrow buttons in the dialog box or the up- and down-arrow keys on your keyboard to change the margin values.

Each measurement you set is for that distance from the edge of the page. For example, if you type 2 in the Top text box, your text begins two inches from the top of the page.

4. Choose OK to close the dialog box.

✔ Use decimals for your measurements in the text boxes. For example, if you want a 1 1/2-inch margin, type **1.5**. If you want a 3/4-inch margin, type **.75**. You don't have to type the inch marks after the numbers. WordPerfect puts them in for you.

✔ If you come from the old school of fraction-users, you can type fractions for your measurements. For example, if you want 1 7/8-inch margins, just type **1 7/8**.

✔ As you change your margins, the little "page" at the right of the dialog box changes to give you a rough idea of how your margins will look.

✔ You only need to set measurements for the margins you want to change. Don't bother re-entering margin measurements if you plan to leave them the same as they were when the dialog box came up.

TIP

Changing margin settings is a good way to increase or decrease the amount of text that fits on a page. If you need more room to fit all your text on a page, make smaller margins—say, 0.75-inch margins instead of 1-inch margins.

College students take note: If you need a document to take up more pages, make your margins a little bigger. Most college professors can't tell the difference between a 1-inch margin and a 1.25-inch margin. Most college professors can, however, tell the difference between a 1-inch margin and a 2-inch margin, so don't take this little deception to the extreme.

"I HATE THIS!"

No 0-inch margins allowed!

If you're using a laser printer, you can't set margins of zero inches because laser printers can't print to the edge of the paper. If you try to set margins of zero inches, WordPerfect will automatically adjust them to your printer's minimum margin capabilities.

Adding Page Numbers

Page numbers are vital for keeping a document in order. Suppose that you copy a 22-page report. Suddenly the copier takes a disliking to the report and spits the pages out in a scrambled order. Without page numbers, all the king's horses and all the king's men won't be able to put the report back together again.

Setting the Page Number

One of the cardinal sins of WordPerfect is numbering pages yourself by typing them at the top (or bottom) of the page. After all, if you have to edit the document, your page numbers can wind up in the wrong places, and even on the wrong pages. Instead, use the WordPerfect automatic page numbering system. Here's how you do it:

1. Move the insertion point to the page you want your page numbering to begin on.

There's one exception to this rule. If you want page numbering to begin on page two, you should still move your insertion point to the beginning of page one and follow these steps; then follow the steps in the first item in the upcoming section, "Page 2 on Page Numbers."

2. Choose **L**ayout, **P**age, **N**umbering to bring up the Page Numbering dialog box.

Click and hold this button for a list of page number positions

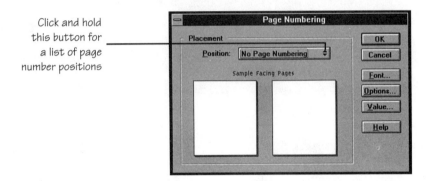

3. Click and hold the button beside **P**osition.

A menu pops up with a list of places where the page number can go.

TIP

For most documents, you can ignore the Alternating **T**op and Alternating **B**ottom options. These are only useful if you're going to have your document bound and printed.

4. Choose an option corresponding to the part of the page that will have page numbers. For example, choose Top **R**ight if you want page numbers in the upper right corner of the pages. Choose Bottom Center if you want page numbers in the bottom center of each page.

5. Choose OK to go back to the document window.

You're all set, page-numbering-wise. If you're using the Draft view mode, the page numbers aren't visible while you type. You can see the page numbers by switching to the Page View mode. (To do this, choose **V**iew, **P**age.) Scroll to the part of the page you put the number on.

Page 2 on Page Numbers

There are lots of things you can do to tinker with the placement of page numbers.

✔ You may not want page numbering to begin until the second page—that's the way things usually work in letters and reports. To start page numbering on the second page, set up page numbering beginning on the first page, and then go to the top of the document. (To go to the top of the document quickly, press Ctrl+Home.) Choose Layout, Page, Suppress; choose Page Numbering; and then choose OK to get back to the document screen. Don't worry; this only stops the page numbering on the first page. Your page numbering will pick up again on the second page.

✔ You can add text next to the page number. For example, the page number could read *Page 3* rather than just *3*. To add text, follow steps 1 through 4 in the basic steps. Before you do step 5, choose Options to bring up the Page Numbering Options dialog box. [Pg #] will be highlighted in the Format and Accompanying Text text box. Press the left-arrow key to move the insertion point to the left of this code. Type the text you want next to the page number, such as **Page**. Press the space bar so that there'll be a space between your text and the page number. Choose OK to close this dialog box, and choose OK again to return to your document.

✔ You can make automatic page numbering part of a WordPerfect header or footer. For instructions (as well as an explanation of "headers" and "footers"), see "Creating Headers and Footers" later in this chapter.

✔ If you want to insert the page number within the text of your document, move the insertion point to where you want the number, and then press Ctrl+Shift+P.

continues

I HATE WORDPERFECT FOR WINDOWS!

Checklist (continued)

✔ If you want automatic page numbering, but need to start at a number different from 1, follow steps 1 through 4; then choose **V**alue to bring up the Numbering Value dialog box. The current page number is highlighted in the New **P**age Number text box. Type the number you want to start with, and then choose OK. Choose OK again to go back to the document.

Centering a Page between Top and Bottom Margins

When you make a cover page for a report, you usually want the text centered between the top and bottom margins. Here's how you center everything on a page between the top and bottom margins:

1. Move the insertion point to the page containing the text you want centered between the top and bottom margins.

2. Choose Layout, **P**age, **C**enter.

The Center Page(s) dialog box appears.

3. Choose the Current **P**age radio button. Or, if you want every page in the rest of the document to be centered, choose Current and Subsequent Pages.

4. Choose OK to return to the document screen.

On the document screen, the page won't look centered between the top and bottom margins if you're using the Draft view mode. Don't worry; it is. If you don't trust WordPerfect, switch to Page View mode, which is discussed in Chapter 8.

TIP

Steps 1 through 4 center the page between the top and bottom margins. If you also want to center the page between the left and right margins, go to the top of the page, and then choose Layout, Justification, Center. You can change back to regular justification after that page by moving to the next page, and then choosing Layout, Justification, Left (or Full).

Creating Headers and Footers

A *header* is text that shows up at the top of every page in a document. A *footer* is the same kind of thing, but it shows up at the bottom of the page—rather than the top. The main purpose of headers and footers is to give your documents continuity. You might, for example, include your company name or the title of your report in the header. The footer might include the date or page number.

Here's how to put a header or footer into your document:

1. Move the insertion point to the first page that you want to have the header.

   If you want the header to start on the first page of the document, press Ctrl+Home.

2. Choose Layout, Header/Footer.

   The Header/Footer dialog box appears.

3. Choose the Header A (if you want text at the *top* of each page) or Footer A (if you want text at the *bottom* of each page) radio button.

4. Choose **Create**.

   An editing window appears that looks a lot like the regular document window. The only difference is a new bar at the top of the screen, with a few buttons on it.

5. Type the text for the header or footer.

   The title of your document, the date it was created, your name, and a page number code are common things to put in headers and footers.

6. After you're done creating the header or footer, choose **File Close** to go back to the document window.

TIP

You can also close the header or footer window by clicking the **C**lose button on the bar that appears when you create the header or footer. Or, if you're working in **P**age mode, just click the mouse pointer below the header (or above the footer).

Header and footer ideas

✔ If you usually work in Draft View mode, you won't be able to see headers and footers while you're writing your document. You can print the document or use the Page View mode to see the header or footer.

✔ If you want the current page number in your header or footer, move the insertion point to where you want the page number, click the **N**umber button on the bar that appears when you're creating a header or footer, and then choose **P**age Number.

✔ You can have the current date as part of the header or footer. Just choose Insert, Date, and then choose Date Code. This date updates automatically whenever you open or print the document.

✔ If you decide you want to make changes to a header or footer you've already created, follow the same steps—except in step 4, choose Edit instead of Create. This takes you into the editing screen where you created the header or footer. Make the changes you need, and then click the Close button in the bar that appears at the top of the Header/Footer editing window.

✔ If you're using Page View mode, you can go back into your header or footer just by clicking the mouse pointer in it. When you're done, click the mouse pointer back in the main part of the page. What could be easier?

✔ If you don't want a header or footer to appear on the first page of a document, go to the top of your document; choose Layout menu, Page; choose Suppress; choose Header A or Footer A; and then choose OK in the dialog box.

✔ You can have headers and footers on each page in your document. You're not restricted to having one or the other.

Adding a Page Border

Occasionally, you might want to put a border around your page to draw a little extra attention. If you need to make your document fancy, read on. If you aren't interested, skip it.

November 15, 1994

824 Rosedale Ct.
Grand Junction, CO 81001

Steven Schmallegar, President
New Moose Cinema, Inc.
468 S. Nixon Blvd.
Orange, CA 82559

Dear Mr. Schmallegar:

I understand that your company is currently shopping around for new scripts. I think I have something you'll like. What I mean to say is, I *know* I have it, but I think you'll like it, if you take my meaning.

I have written a screenplay (enclosed) based on Fyodor Dostoevsky's famous whodunit novel *Crime and Punishment*. I know, I know, that's not exactly a new idea. But here's the twist, Mr. Schmalllegar, and I think you'll agree that this *is* new: *It's a musical.*

"Why a musical?" you're certainly entitled to ask. Well, I've always thought that the novel is just too darn dark—not to mention esoteric—as it stands, for most people, anyway. Sure, the modern audience wants culture, but they also want entertainment—something that'll put a little bounce in their step.

Imagine Raskolnikov as he contemplates murdering the old pawnshop woman. Instead of just stewing and muttering to himself, he breaks into song, something that both conveys his inner turmoil *and* makes us want to tap our toes.

I could go on and on, Mr. Schmallegar, but I think you've got the idea. I hope you're as excited about the project as I.

Sincerely,

Howard Beighfey

Howard Beighfey

P.S. Perhaps with the recent successful animated adaptations of various classic stories, we should consider making this an *animated* musical. I look forward to hearing from you.

Artsy page border

Here are the steps for adding a border:

1. Move the insertion point to the page you want a border around. It doesn't really matter where on the page. Just somewhere on it.

2. Choose Layout, Page, Border/Fill. The Page Border dialog box appears.

3. Click on the big square button—the one that reads NO BORDER—by Border Style.

A bunch of different types of borders appear, ranging from the simple and elegant to the unspeakably ugly.

4. Find a border that you like and click on it.

The border you chose appears on the sample page to the right of the document. If you don't like the border after all, repeat steps 3 and 4 to change it.

5. Choose OK.

The border is just outside the margins. You can get a good look at it by printing the page or by clicking the Zoom Full Page button on the Power Bar.

"I HATE THIS!"

I didn't want *all* my pages to have borders!

After you follow these steps, every page from this point forward in your document will have a border. If you don't like this effect, move the insertion point so that it's somewhere in the first page where you *don't* want the border. Choose Layout, Page, Border/Fill. Click the big square button by Border Style, and then choose the NO BORDER option. Choose OK to go back to your document window. All pages from this point forward *won't* have a border around them.

EXPERTS ONLY

I only want a border around a *paragraph!*

If you have a certain paragraph (or any amount of text, really) in your document that is absolutely positively critically important for your audience to read, put a border around it.

Select the text you want to border. Choose **L**ayout, **P**aragraph, **B**order/Fill to bring up the Paragraph Border dialog box. From here, you create the border the same as if you were creating a border for the whole page.

The Label Maker

Labels are great for sticking on envelopes, packages, folders, diskettes, whatever. Avery makes a size of label for just about anything you might want to put a label on. The trouble with labels is that it has always been almost impossibly difficult to get the computer to print on the right place on them. You tend to wind up with the text halfway on the label, and halfway off.

WordPerfect for Windows finally makes it easy to print labels from your computer. You just tell WordPerfect which size label you're using, and then type away. When you print, WordPerfect will see to it that your text winds up on the labels.

TIP

There's a good reason why you should use Avery labels when you use WordPerfect. WordPerfect knows Avery labels and has a customized label setup for every kind of Avery label. No matter which Avery label you have, you know WordPerfect will work with it.

Here's how to create a sheet—or more—of labels:

1. Begin with a blank document window.

You can choose **File, New** to get a new document window, or you can close any other document windows you're working on.

2. Choose **Layout, Labels** to bring up the Labels dialog box.

Choose your label type from this list

Type of printer the label works with

Sketch of how the labels sit on the page

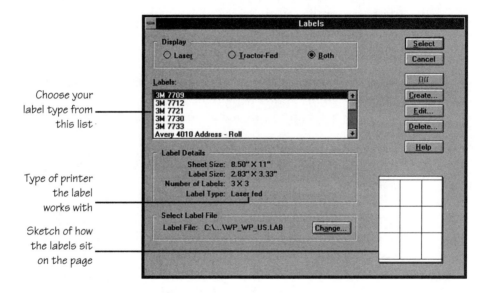

3. Scroll through the Labels list box to find the type of label you're using, and make sure that the label type is highlighted.

All Avery labels have an identifying number printed on the box. Look for this number in the list.

When you've highlighted a label type, check the sketch of the label type in the lower right corner of the dialog box—it should be divided in the same way your labels are divided. Also, make sure that the Label Type is set to the kind of printer you use.

4. Choose Select.

5. Type the information that goes on each label. Press Ctrl+Enter between each label to tell WordPerfect to start a new label.

✔ WordPerfect labels *don't* go all the way down a column, and then start again at the top of the next column; they go from left to right. As you type your labels, expect to use all the first row first, then the next row, and so on.

✔ If you're printing labels with a laser printer, don't send the same page through the printer more than once or twice. Otherwise, the label page will start to curl and is more likely to jam in the printer.

✔ If you decide to print a few labels on a sheet, and then print a few more later on, you may be wondering how to get WordPerfect to start on the seventh or eighth label, instead of the first. Well, follow the preceding steps normally, through step 4. Then press Ctrl+Enter as many times as you need to move down to a label that hasn't been used. For example, if the first five labels have been used, you would press Ctrl+Enter five times to get to the sixth label. You can check the status bar to see which page you're on. (When you're working in labels, each label is considered its own page.)

CHAPTER 13

A Place for Everything, and Everything in Its Place

IN A NUTSHELL

▼ Change your tab stops

▼ Make sure that certain parts of your document stay together on the same page

▼ Clean up your document with the Reveal Codes feature

I HATE WORDPERFECT FOR WINDOWS!

f you're finicky, you will love this chapter, which is about setting tabs to keep things in order. You also will learn how to keep certain paragraphs or other text on the same page—for the sake of neatness, of course. And, for the grand finale, you will learn about Reveal Codes, the ultimate WordPerfect clean-up feature.

If you aren't so finicky—if your office is so messy that you are considering fire-bombing it to get rid of the clutter—you still might find this information interesting. WordPerfect makes it easy to keep everything lined up perfectly.

Changing Tab Stops

If you aren't particular about where tabbed text lines up, use the default tab settings (a tab stop every half inch). If you want the text indented more than a half-inch, press Tab again to move over another half inch. Keep pressing Tab until the text is indented as far as you want it.

If you *are* picky about where tabs line up and you *don't* like extraneous tabs in the text (you want a tab at 2.8 inches and you want one—and only one—tab stop), you can use a group of tab stops called *tab settings*.

You can have several different tab settings in a document, and each setting applies until you change tab settings again or until the end of the document—whichever comes first.

Making the Switch

Here's how to set a new tab setting:

1. Move the insertion point to the beginning of the line where you want the new tab setting to begin.

If you want the tab setting to be in effect for the whole document, press Ctrl+Home to move the insertion point to the beginning of the document.

2. Choose **V**iew, **R**uler Bar.

The Ruler appears on-screen, showing all your tab stops.

The Ruler

Tab stops on the Ruler

Click on the spot where you want a tab

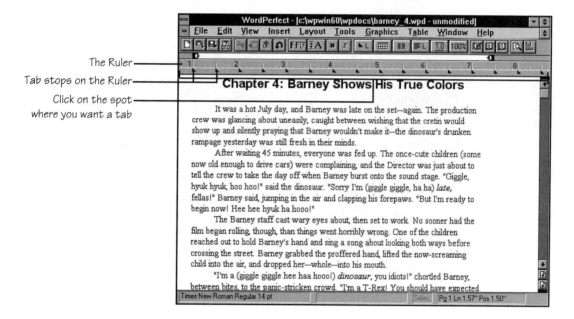

3. Make any changes to your tab setting. Choose **V**iew, **R**uler Bar again to make the Ruler go away.

The following checklist covers some of the exciting things you can do with the Ruler.

✔ To add a tab stop, just click on the Ruler where you want a tab.

✔ To move a tab stop, click on an existing tab, and then drag it to its new position. As you drag the tab stop, a dotted line goes down the screen—following your mouse pointer—showing where text tabbed to that position will go.

✔ If you're dragging a tab stop and change your mind about moving it, just drag the mouse pointer above the Ruler before releasing the mouse button. The tab stop will remain in its original position.

✔ To remove a tab, click it and drag it off the Ruler.

✔ If you want to remove *all* the tabs from the Ruler, click and hold the Power Bar's Ruler pop-up button, and then choose Clear All Tabs.

✔ If you want to be very specific about where a tab goes, use the Tab Set dialog box. Choose Layout, Line, **T**ab Set (or just double-click a tab stop in the Ruler). In the **P**osition box, type the position from the left margin you want the tab to be, in inches. Choose **S**et. You can keep adding tab stops this way. When you've added the last one, choose OK.

✔ You might want to put tab stops at regular intervals on the Tab Ruler—say, for instance, every quarter inch. You do this from the Tab Set dialog box. Choose Layout, Line, **T**ab Set to get this dialog box. Choose Clear **A**ll to get rid of the existing tab stops. In the **P**osition box, type the distance from the left margin where you want the first tab. Next, check the Repeat Every check box and type the distance that should be between each tab stop. If you want tab stops every quarter-inch (0.25") and want the first one to begin at the left margin, type 0 in the **P**osition box (so that the tab stop

will be zero inches from the left margin), choose the Repeat Every check box, type **.25** in the Repeat Every box, and then choose OK. (It's really easy once you get used to how WordPerfect thinks.)

✔ If you need to change tab sets often in a document, you can display the Ruler while you write. Just make sure that the insertion point is where you want the tab set to take effect whenever you start changing tabs.

Using Fancy Tab Stops

While you will almost always want to use normal tabs, WordPerfect also has other kinds. You put other tabs on the tab Ruler by clicking and holding on the Power Bar's Tab Set pop up button, choosing the type of tab you want to use, and then clicking on the Ruler where you want the tab. Once you have selected a tab type, you can add as many as you like to the Ruler. Here are the kinds of tabs you can select from the Ruler:

Choose This	Important Stuff about the Tab
◣ Left	This is the normal type of tab. When you tab to a left tab stop, text that comes after the tab flows to the right.
▲ Center	When you tab to a center tab stop, the text you type is centered over that tab, not centered between the margins. Use this type of tab for column headings.
◢ Right	When you tab to a right tab stop, the text you type flows to the left, which means the *end* of your text is at the tab stop. Use this type of tab for headings that appear above columns of numbers.

continues

Choose This	Important Stuff about the Tab
⬟ Decimal	Use this type when you need to type a column of numbers with decimals. All of your numbers will line up on the decimal point, making things easier to add.
⬟ ⬟ ⬟ ⬟	These tab stops work like regular left, center, right, or decimal tabs, but when you tab to this type of tab stop, a row of dots appears from your previous position to the beginning of the tab, like this:

```
             Recipes for Success......123
```

Keeping Text on the Same Page
(All together now)

Once in a while you will have a pair of paragraphs that you want on the same page, no matter what. Or you might have a list of items that you don't want split between pages. Here's what you do:

1. Select the entire section you want to keep from being divided.

2. Choose Layout, Page, Keep Text Together.

The Keep Text Together dialog box appears.

3. Choose the check box labeled **Keep** selected text together on same page.

4. Choose OK.

If WordPerfect would have put a page break in the area you selected, the page break now comes before the block so that the section isn't split between pages.

EXPERTS ONLY

How to protect widows and orphans

It's a real WordPerfect *faux pas* for the last line of a paragraph be the first line on a page. It's equally gauche for the first line of a paragraph to be on the last line of the page—those lines look so sad and lonely.

Those stray lines are called widows and orphans, and the Keep Text Together dialog box can keep them out of your documents. Just move your insertion point to the beginning of the document; choose Layout, Page, Keep Text Together; select the check box in the Widow/Orphan group; and then choose OK. WordPerfect will make sure your document is widow- and orphan-free.

Erasing Unwanted Formatting

Reveal Codes. What an ominous term—well-named because it *is* ominous.

When you make formatting changes—make words bold or italic, change margins, add headers and footers—WordPerfect is putting codes into your document.

These codes are notes WordPerfect makes to itself: "Start bold here and end it here; Put a header here; Change the margins here." Usually you can't see these codes because they'd just get in the way of your work; but when you turn on Reveal Codes, you can see all the codes that have been inserted into your document—as if you had turned a big X-ray on your document.

Looking at the Dark World of Reveal Codes

When would you want to see your codes? When you want to delete one, mainly. Some formatting features are hard to remove from your document unless you can see the formatting code. In that case, you have to travel into the dark world of Reveal Codes.

Turning on Reveal Codes (Brace yourself!)

To turn on Reveal Codes, choose **View**, Reveal Codes.

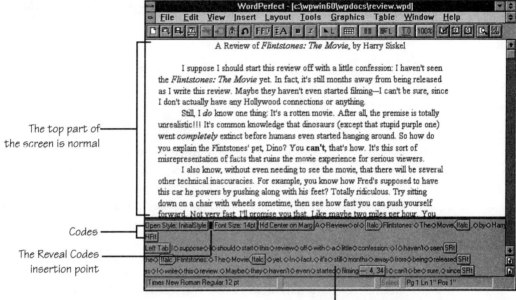

The top part of the screen is normal

Codes

The Reveal Codes insertion point

The bottom part of the screen shows Reveal Codes

When you turn on Reveal Codes, a bar splits the screen in two. The top part of the screen is the normal document screen while the bottom part of the screen is the Reveal Codes area. In this dark and mysterious world, your spaces appear as diamonds, and every code appears as a button. Rectangular buttons are normal codes that mark where a certain feature takes effect. Buttons that point in one direction or another are called "paired codes," and you'll learn about these monstrosities a little later in this chapter.

I HATE WORDPERFECT FOR WINDOWS!

✔ You can turn off Reveal Codes by choosing **V**iew, Reveal **C**odes.

✔ If you begin to like Reveal Codes so much that you want to be able to turn it on at a second's notice, use the Alt+F3 shortcut. The same key combo also turns off Reveal Codes.

✔ You can change the amount of space Reveal Codes takes by moving the mouse pointer to the top of Reveal Codes. When the pointer turns into an up-and-down arrow, click and drag the top bar of Reveal Codes to the desired height. You can also turn off Reveal Codes by using this technique to drag the Reveal Codes bar all the way to the bottom of the WordPerfect window.

✔ You can do anything within the Reveal Codes window that you can do on the document screen. You can type, erase, and move around, but it's a nuisance because you have to dodge all the codes. Why bother?

✔ If you don't know what a code does, leave it alone. Don't erase a code unless you know its purpose.

✔ As you move the insertion point in the document window, a little black rectangle moves in the Reveal Codes section. This rectangle shows where the insertion point is positioned in Reveal Codes.

✔ You can click the mouse pointer anywhere in Reveal Codes and the Reveal Codes insertion point will move to that spot, just like clicking your mouse pointer in the regular editing window.

Meeting the Popular HRt and SRt Codes

More than any other code, you'll see a lot of HRt and SRt codes in the Reveal Codes screen. HRt is the code for *hard return*. WordPerfect puts one of these in your document whenever you press Enter.

SRt is WordPerfect's code for a *soft return*—the end of a line. Whenever you're typing and the insertion point jumps down to the next line, WordPerfect puts one of these SRt codes at the end of the line you just finished.

CAUTION

Don't try to delete SRt codes; WordPerfect put them there for a good reason. If you move your cursor to the left of an SRt code and press Delete, it's like deleting the space between two words: the words on the left and right of the SRt you deleted will be joined.

Housecleaning with Reveal Codes

The main reason to use Reveal Codes is to delete formatting changes you don't want in your document. You might want to delete line spacing changes, for example. To do this, you need to find the line spacing code. Move the insertion point to the right of the code you want to erase. Press Backspace. The code disappears, and so does the formatting.

Many of the codes in WordPerfect are called *paired codes*. These codes come in twos. Instead of being perfectly rectangular, paired codes point toward each other. The first of these two codes points to the right and turns on a feature; the second points left and turns off the feature. The Bold feature uses paired codes. Before any bold text, you see Bold On in a box pointing right. At the end of the bold text is the second of the paired code set: Bold Off, pointing left. When you delete either of the paired codes, the other also disappears.

TIP

If you're using your mouse, there are a couple of cool tricks you can do in Reveal Codes. To get rid of a code you don't want, just click it, drag it down to the bottom of the screen, and release the mouse button. If you want to edit the formatting made by a code (say, for instance, you see a margin code and you want to change the margin), just double-click the code and WordPerfect takes you to the dialog box that makes that code. You can then change the formatting that made the code.

EXPERTS ONLY

Stripping all instances of a code from a document

You can use the Replace feature to strip all of a certain type of formatting from your document. You can remove all the bold, or all the tabs, or all the margin changes, or all the line spacing changes. Or any other type of code you want to strip. You can do this with Reveal Codes on or off.

Move the insertion point to the point where you want to begin removing the formatting. (To begin at the top of the document, press Ctrl+Home.) Choose **Edit**, **Replace**. Choose **Match**, **Codes** from the dialog box's menu to get a list of codes you can remove. Highlight the code you want to take out of your document, and then choose Insert. This doesn't mean you're inserting the code into your document; it just means that you're inserting the code into the dialog box so that you can remove it from your document. For example, to strip underlining from your document, highlight Und On (which is WordPerfect's secret code for "Underline On"), and then choose Insert. Choose Close to close the Codes dialog box.

Here's the real trick: you now leave the Replace With text box empty so that WP searches for your code and replaces it with nothing. Choose Replace All to move all the instances of the code. WordPerfect strips all the formatting that you specified. Choose Close to return to the document screen. If you decide that it was a big mistake to do all that code removal, choose Edit, Undo right away to bring it all back.

Reveal Codes Revealed

Here are some of the most common Reveal Codes:

What the Code Says	What the Code Means
HRt	Hard Return. You pressed Enter here.
SRt	Soft Return. WordPerfect is wrapping the line here.
HPg	Hard Page. You pressed Ctrl+Enter to end the page here.
SPg	Soft Page. WordPerfect ends the page here. Don't erase this!
Left Tab	Text moves in one tab stop here.
Hd Left Ind	Paragraph is indented one tab stop here.

continues

What the Code Says	What the Code Means
Hd Back Tab	Text moves back one tab stop here.
Und	Underline paired codes that mark the beginning and end of <u>underlined</u> text.
Bold	Bold paired codes that mark the beginning and end of **bold** text.
Italc	Italic paired codes that mark the beginning and end of *italic* text.
Fine	Fine text size paired codes that mark the beginning and end of very small text.
Small	Small text size paired codes that mark the beginning and end of small text.
Large	Large paired codes that mark the beginning and end of large text.
Very Large	Very Large text size paired codes that mark the beginning and end of very large text.
Ext Large	Extra Large text size paired codes that mark the beginning and end of extra large text.
Hd Center on Marg	A centered line begins here.
Hd Flush Right	A line begins here that is flush with the right margin.

What the Code Says	What the Code Means
Just: Right	All text is flush with the right margin until further notice.
Just: Full	All text is flush against both margins until further notice.
Just: Cntr	All text is centered between the left and right margins until further notice.
Just: Left	All text is flush with left margin—but not the right margin—until further notice.
Lft Mar: 1.50"	New left margin goes into effect here. The number is the new margin. (Note that your on-screen numbers might be different.)
Rgt Mar: 1.50"	New right margin goes into effect here. The number is the new margin. (Note that your on-screen numbers might be different.)
Top Mar: 1.50"	New top margin goes into effect here. The number is the new margin. (Note that your on-screen numbers might be different.)
Bot Mar: 1.50"	New bottom margin goes into effect here. The number is the new margin. (Note that your on-screen numbers might be different.)

continues

I HATE WORDPERFECT FOR WINDOWS!

What the Code Says	What the Code Means
Tab Set: (*numbers here*)	New tab set goes into effect here. The numbers are the tab stop locations and are almost impossible to decipher.
Cntr Cur Pg: On	Page is centered between top to bottom margins.
Header A: Every Page	Header A begins here. (A similar code is available for footers.)
Pg Num Pos: TopRight	Page numbering goes into effect here.
Font:Times	Indicated font starts here.
Font Size:12pt	New font size starts here.

TIP

Every document begins with an Open Style: InitialStyle code. Don't bother trying to delete it; you can't. It's just there, and no amount of pressing Delete and Backspace will change it. This code tells WordPerfect any special permanent changes you've made to your line spacing, margins, and so forth.

CHAPTER 14

Creating a Form Letter

(Dear Fill-in-the-Blank)

IN A NUTSHELL

▼ Make a list of the names and addresses of the recipients

▼ Create the form letter

▼ Merge the letter and the list

S uppose that you need to send the same letter out to lots of people. On one hand, you want to send out a personalized letter, not a generic one. On the other hand, you don't want to type the same letter over and over. Is there a solution? Yes—WordPerfect's mighty Merge feature.

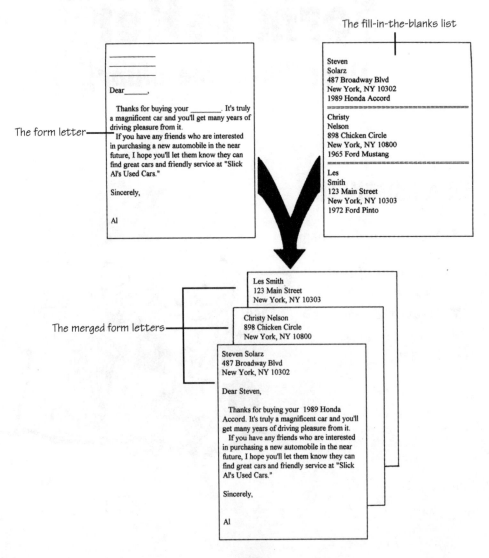

The fill-in-the-blanks list

The form letter

```
_____
_____
_____

Dear_____,

    Thanks for buying your _____. It's truly
a magnificent car and you'll get many years of
driving pleasure from it.
    If you have any friends who are interested
in purchasing a new automobile in the near
future, I hope you'll let them know they can
find great cars and friendly service at "Slick
Al's Used Cars."

Sincerely,


Al
```

```
Steven
Solarz
487 Broadway Blvd
New York, NY 10302
1989 Honda Accord
================================
Christy
Nelson
898 Chicken Circle
New York, NY 10800
1965 Ford Mustang
================================
Les
Smith
123 Main Street
New York, NY 10303
1972 Ford Pinto
```

The merged form letters

```
Les Smith
123 Main Street
New York, NY 10303
```

```
Christy Nelson
898 Chicken Circle
New York, NY 10800
```

```
Steven Solarz
487 Broadway Blvd
New York, NY 10302

Dear Steven,

    Thanks for buying your  1989 Honda
Accord. It's truly a magnificent car and you'll
get many years of driving pleasure from it.
    If you have any friends who are interested
in purchasing a new automobile in the near
future, I hope you'll let them know they can
find great cars and friendly service at "Slick
Al's Used Cars."

Sincerely,


Al
```

The idea behind Merge is to make a list of fill-in-the-blank information, like the names and addresses of people you want to send a letter. When writing the letter, simply leave blanks to be filled in later. With the magic of WordPerfect's Merge feature, you combine the two documents, making a (heh, heh) "personal" letter to each person.

This chapter shows you how to work the Merge magic. If you don't need to send form letters, skip this chapter. If you do, read on. The process may seem scary, but it's much easier and less painful than typing the same letter 50 times.

A Quick Preview

To create a personalized form letter, you need two documents: the data list and the form. The *data list* contains all the personal information you want to insert, such as the list of names and addresses that you will use.

BUZZWORDS

FIELD

A *field* is a special code that you insert into your main document. The field tells WordPerfect where to insert personal text.

The *form* is the standard text you want to send to everyone. This document also includes secret codes (called *fields*) that tell WordPerfect, "Insert something personal from the data list here."

Creating the Data List (Fill-in-the-blanks)

You'll want to include certain custom information—such as the person's name and address—in each form letter. The *data list* contains that customized information.

Two steps are involved when making the fill-in-the-blanks list (the data list). First, you tell WordPerfect what kind of information will be in the list. Second, you type the information for each person.

What Do You Want in the List? (Field of dreams)

You can have all kinds of information in the data list (the name and address, of course, but other things, too). You might want to have the last date the person bought something from you, the person's spouse's name, or how much money they owe you. Whatever. Begin by telling WordPerfect what information you'll be putting into the list. Here's how:

1. Choose **T**ools, **M**erge to bring up the Merge dialog box.

2. Choose the **D**ata button. The Create Data File dialog box appears with the insertion point positioned in the **N**ame a Field text box.

If the document window you were using already has text in it, a box appears, asking if you want to use a new document. Choose the **N**ew Document Window radio button, and then choose OK.

3. Type a word that describes the first type of information you want in your list, and then press Enter.

Do this for each type of information you want in the list. Give each one a unique name so that WordPerfect can tell one from another. Think of a word that describes the kind of information you want in

each spot, such as *first name* or *address*. Press Enter after typing each one. Suppose that you want to have the recipient's first name, last name, street address, city, state, and ZIP, and the make of car they bought. You would type **First Name**, press Enter; type **Last Name**, press Enter; type **Street Address**, press Enter; type **City, ST ZIP**, press Enter; and type **Make, Model**, and press Enter. As you type each item and press Enter, that item appears in the **Field Name List** box.

Type these field names in the order that you want to type the information in the list. If you will type the first name, last name, address, and then phone number, type the field names in that same order.

4. When you're finished typing the field names, choose OK.

The prompt disappears, and a dialog box appears on-screen, looking something like this:

WordPerfect creates a text box for each type of information that you'll have in your fill-in-the-blanks list.

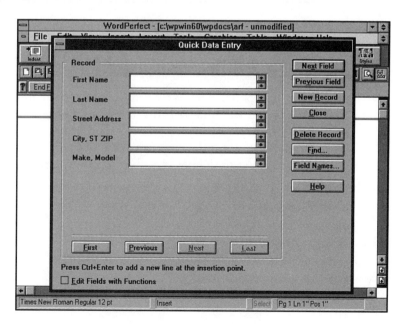

✔ Keep your field names short—one or two words. If they're any longer, they will cause problems later.

✔ If you find you have mistyped one of the field names, click it in the Field **N**ames list box. The field name will appear in the **F**ield Name text box, where you can correct it. Choose **R**eplace to put the corrected version in the list.

✔ If you decide you don't want one of the field names, click it in the Field **N**ames list box, and then choose **D**elete.

✔ If you plan to address people by first name in your letter, you should have separate First Name and Last Name field names. That way, you can use the names apart or together. If you'll never use anything but the full name in your form letter, just have a Name field.

Make the Fill-in-the-Blanks List

The ugly part is over. Now you simply type the information for each letter. You will find that this step is amazingly easy.

Type the text for the current field, and then press Enter. The insertion point moves to the next text box, where you're ready to enter another piece of information.

Sometimes you will come to a column where you don't have anything to type for a certain person. When this happens, just press Enter to skip that field, leaving it blank.

After you've typed all the fill-in-the-blank information about one person, you've created a "record." You're ready to start over, typing the same kind of information about the next person who will receive the letter. When you press Enter in the last text box, the insertion point jumps back to the first text box, so you're ready to begin again.

BUZZWORDS

RECORD

A record is all the custom information about one person in a fill-in-the-blanks list. Each record will have one or more fields. You can have as many records in a data file as you like.

When you're done typing in the custom information you want for everyone, choose **Close**. A box appears, asking Save changes to disk? Choose **Yes**. The Save As dialog box appears. Here you can type a name for the list you have made—make sure you remember the name because you will need it later. You can now close the document window.

"I HATE THIS!"

What's this mess on the screen?

After you have typed all your custom information for the data list and saved it to disk, you're left at a window with all kinds of strange, sinister-looking codes. This mess is your data list. Fortunately, you never have to work with it in this form—it's much easier to use the Quick Data Entry dialog box.

✔ You might need more than one line of text in a field. For example, the street address might take a couple of lines, not just one. To put a second line in a field, press Ctrl+Enter.

✔ If you want to move back to a field you have already typed, either click in that text box or click on the Previous Field button until you're in the right text box.

✔ You can look at records you have already created by clicking the First, Previous, Next, and Last buttons at the bottom of the dialog box. The First button takes you to the first record you typed, Last takes you to the last one you typed, and so on.

✔ If you decide you don't want a record in the list after all, make sure that the record is showing in the text boxes; then choose Delete Record.

✔ You can come back to the Quick Data Entry dialog box later to add, change, or remove records. Just open the data list into a document window, and then click the Quick Entry button that appears in the bar at the top of the window. You return right back at the Quick Data Entry dialog box. After you make your changes and choose Close, you will be asked whether to save your changes. Choose Yes.

Creating the Form Letter

The form is the part of the letter that's the same for everybody who receives a copy. You need to tell WordPerfect you're creating a form. Here's how:

1. Choose **T**ools, **M**erge. The Merge dialog box appears.

2. In the Merge dialog box, choose **F**orm. (If you aren't at a blank document window, a box comes up asking whether to use a new file. Select the **N**ew Document Window radio button, and then choose OK.)

The Create Form File dialog box appears, with the insertion point positioned in the **A**ssociate a Data File text box.

3. Click the folder button to the right of the Associate a Data File text box. The Select File dialog box appears.

4. Scroll through the list of files until you find the name of your data file.

5. Double-click the data file to go back to the Create Form File dialog box. Then choose OK.

From here, you create the form in about the same way you create any other document. Simply type away. But here's the key: where you want to insert *personal* information, you insert a field code. You might want the letter to begin *Dear John*. Type the word *Dear* (and then press a space bar) because it is unchanging text that will be in every letter.

However, you don't want *John* in each letter (unless, of course, everyone you're sending the letter to is named John, which isn't likely). Instead, you want WordPerfect to insert a different name for each letter. To tell WordPerfect to insert a name from a second document, you insert a field code instead of typing **John**.

Here's how you insert field codes:

1. Move the insertion point to where you want the field.

Common places for fields are the address and the greeting.

2. Click the Insert Field Name button in the bar at the top of the document window—just below the Power Bar.

This bar is called the *Merge Feature* bar. It appears whenever you're working with the Merge feature, to give you some shortcuts.

The Select Field Name dialog box appears. This dialog box is where you tell WordPerfect which customized information you want to include.

3. Double-click the field you want to use.

If, for example, you want the first name to appear after the word *Dear*, you would double-click *First Name*.

The field appears in your document, looking something like the following:

```
FIELD(First Name)
```

FIELD always signals the beginning of your field, and the text between the parentheses is the name of the field.

CAUTION

It's not good enough to just type **FIELD(Field Name)** into the document screen. You need to follow these steps or the merge won't work.

4. Continue typing your form letter, double-clicking field names where you want that customized information in your letter.

If the Select Field Name dialog box starts to get in your way, choose its Close button. You can always bring it back by following step 2.

The form file should look something like this:

Merge Feature Bar —
Field codes —

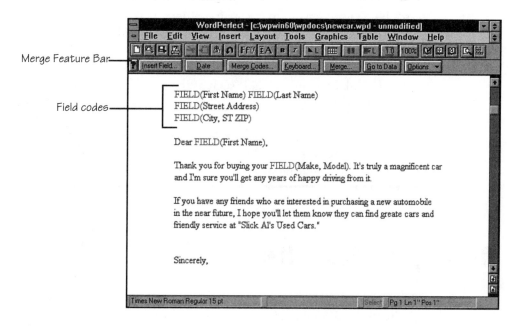

5. When you're finished creating the form letter, save it like you would any document, and then close the document. Be sure that you remember the name you used to save this form file!

Checklist

✔ You can use a field more than once in a document. If you want to use someone's first name several times in a document, just insert a FIELD(First Name) code in each place you want the first name. Sweepstakes letters often insert the name several times:

> You, Bart, might have won a lot of money. That's right, Bart, you could already be a winner...

continues

✔ If you want a word to come after a field, make sure that you include a space after the closing parenthesis in the field. If you want the field to be the last thing in a sentence, make sure that the period comes right after the closing parenthesis. And if you want a couple of blank lines after a field (such as the address field), make sure that you press Enter a couple of times after the field.

✔ You can have fields side by side, like FIELD (First Name) FIELD (Last Name), so that the names are side by side. Just make sure there's a separating space between them.

Merging the Two Letters

So you have made your form letter and your fill-in-the-blanks list. Now you're ready to combine the two into your personalized, customized, gee-whiz, merged letters.

Follow these steps to combine your data list and form letter into a merge-bonanza:

1. Choose **T**ools, Merge. The Merge dialog box appears.

2. In the Merge dialog box, choose the **Merge** button.

The Perform Merge dialog box appears. Here's where you tell WordPerfect the names of the form and data list files that you want to combine.

3. In the **F**orm File text box, type the name of your form letter.

For example, if you were making a form letter to clients who hadn't paid up, you might have named your form letter DEADBEAT. In that case, you would type **DEADBEAT** here, and then press Enter.

Now WordPerfect wants to know the name of your fill-in-the-blanks list.

4. In the Data File text box, type the name of your fill-in-the-blanks list file.

Often, WordPerfect can tell from the Form File you're using which Data File you want to use, so you may not have to type anything here—it may be filled in automatically for you.

5. Choose OK.

A `Please Wait` box appears in the middle of the screen, counting off the form letters it's merging. This prompt lets you know that WordPerfect is busy combining your two files.

When the merge is done, all your personalized form letters are in one document with page breaks separating each letter.

Checklist

✔ If you can't remember the name of the data or form file, click the button beside the text box and choose Select File from the menu that appears. A dialog box appears; find the name, and then double-click it.

✔ If you have an especially large fill-in-the-blanks list, the merge could take a while.

✔ The document created by your merge doesn't have a name. If you want to keep the document, you need to save it.

TIP

You can have WordPerfect send all your form letters straight to the printer instead of into one giant document. Follow steps 1 through 4, click the button beside the Output File text box, and then choose <Printer> from the menu that pops up. Choose OK to start the Merge. Make sure that you've got plenty of paper in the printer!

Envelopes for Your Letters

So you would like nice printed envelopes to go along with those form letters? No problem, as long as you know how to load envelopes into your printer. But there are quite a few steps, and it's not for the weak of heart, so take a deep breath and follow along.

To print an envelope for each form letter, follow steps 1 through 4 in the previous section. Then choose the **Envelopes** button at the bottom of the dialog box. The Envelope dialog box appears, and the insertion point is positioned in the **Mailing Address** text box.

Choose the Fields button at the bottom of the dialog box to see a list of your available fields. Double-click the first field you want on the envelope—the First Name field, for instance. Add a space (or new line). Click the Fields button again to bring up the Select Field Name dialog box.

Continue this process until you've got all the field names the merge will need to make a good address. For example, your text in the **Mailing Addresses** text box might wind up looking like this:

```
FIELD (First Name) FIELD (Last Name)
FIELD (Street Address)
FIELD (City, ST ZIP)
```

If you aren't using preprinted envelopes, you should also type your return address. Click in the **R**eturn Addresses text box and type your return address.

Once everything is set in this dialog box, choose OK to go back to the Perform Merge dialog box, and then choose OK to start the merge.

When the merge is finished, your letters are at the top of the document and the corresponding envelopes are at the bottom. When you print this document, the printer will pause when it gets to the envelopes, letting you insert the envelopes to be printed, unless you have a special feeder for the envelopes, in which case the envelopes should just start printing by themselves.

Getting envelopes to print, by the way, is the single most difficult thing to do with a computer printer. If you have trouble getting the envelopes to come out right—or come out at all—get your local computer guru to help.

CHAPTER 15

Using Lines In Your Documents

(Line Up!)

IN A NUTSHELL

▼ Create lines

▼ Move lines with the mouse

▼ Change the line's length and thickness with the mouse

▼ Remove unwanted lines and wrinkles

One of the easiest ways to give your pages a little pizzazz is to strategically place lines on the page. Lines at the top and bottom of the page give documents a classy, typeset look. A vertical line—strategically placed—can give your document a unique look. You can also use lines to create unique designs that you can then sell for lots of money at local art shows. Or you can use them like this:

This flyer uses horizontal lines to set off important sections of information. It also uses vertical and horizontal lines to make the tic-tac-toe boards.

A N N O U N C I N G
The Fifth Annual Idaho

Tic-
Tac-
Toe

C H A M P I O N S H I P S

Where: Moscow Civic Center

When: Saturday, July 23: 8:00 a.m. — 9:30 p.m.

Why: To see some of the best Tic-Tac-Toe strategy on the face of this earth! If you think the Spring Potato Grow-Off was a hoot, wait'll you see this!

Making Lines

Lines are great for separating headers and footers from the rest of the document. They're useful in resumes for separating your name and address from the body of the document. They're also perfect to use if you want to show the brain activity of a rutabaga.

To create a line, just choose Graphics; then choose Horizontal Line or Vertical Line. The line appears on-screen. If you're creating a horizontal line, the line appears at the same height as the insertion point, going from the left margin to the right margin. If you're creating a vertical line, the line appears at the left margin, going from the top to the bottom margin.

TIP

Vertical lines look good between columns—but there's a much easier and better way to put them there than using Graphic Lines. Read Chapter 17 to find out how.

Checklist

✔ If you want a line to separate the header from the rest of the document, put the line *inside* the header. While you're in the header edit window, create the header. (See Chapter 12 for all the dirt on creating headers.) Then press Ctrl+End; press Enter to go to a new line; and then choose Graphics, Horizontal Line to make the line. Choose File, Close to go to the document window.

✔ To use a line to separate a footer from the rest of the document, you follow the same steps as in creating a header, but you want the line at the *top* of the text; press Ctrl+Home to move the insertion

continues

point to the top of the document. Choose Graphics, Horizontal Line. Then press Enter twice to keep the line from sitting right on top of the text.

✔ You can change the line's length, thickness, position, and look. Learn how in the next two sections in this chapter.

If you want a border around the page or a paragraph, don't do it with lines. Instead, see Chapter 12. That chapter teaches you how to make classy-looking borders.

Moving and Sizing the Lines

With the mouse, it's a cinch to put your lines just where you want them, and just as easy to make them the right length and thickness.

Start by selecting the line: Move the mouse pointer so that the tip of it is on the line; then click. The line is now selected and looks like the bottom line shown here:

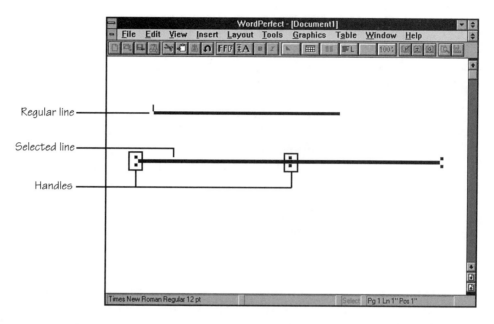

Regular line

Selected line

Handles

"I HATE THIS!"

Argh! I can't select the line!

It's hard to select those thin little lines. You may have to move the mouse just slightly and try clicking again a couple of times before you can get it selected.

BUZZWORDS

HANDLES

The little black boxes at different places around the selected line are called *handles*. By clicking on the handles and dragging, you can change the thickness and length of the line.

I HATE WORDPERFECT FOR WINDOWS!

Checklist

✔ To move the line, move the mouse so that it's somewhere inside the line. The mouse pointer turns to a four-way arrow, and you can click and drag the line to wherever you want it.

✔ To size the line, click on the little black handle for the direction you want to stretch the line, and then drag the mouse. For instance, suppose that you have a vertical line, and you want to make it thicker. You would click the handle on the right side of the line, and then drag it to the right.

✔ If you want to change the length and thickness of a line at the same time, click on one of the line's corner handles. That way, you can drag up and down, as well as left and right, to change the line's size in any way you want.

✔ It's good to be able to see the whole page when you're working with lines—especially when you're moving the line. Click the Full Page Zoom button on the Power Bar to see the whole page while you're working with lines; then click it again to go back to how you were working.

EXPERTS ONLY

Fussy line placement

If you want to be very precise in the placement of your line and how long it is, use the Edit Graphic Line dialog box. Double-click the line you want to change to bring up the dialog box. In the Position/Length group box, make sure that the Horizontal pop-up menu has Set selected (click the button and drag to Set); then type the horizontal position you want the line to start at—this is the distance from the left edge of the page. Next, make sure that the Vertical

pop-up menu has Set selected, and type the distance from the top of the page you want the line to start. Finally, in the Length text box, type how long you want the line to be. If you want to change how thick the line is, type the new thickness in the Thickness box (which is hidden down at the bottom right of the dialog box).

As you make all these changes, a little preview screen in the upper right corner of the dialog box shows you how your line will look on the page. Choose OK when you're done making your nit-picky changes.

Customizing Your Line's Look

What?! A plain, simple, single line isn't good enough for you? You want something fancier? Something with a little zip? Well, you want to *customize* your lines, then.

Here's how you customize a line:

1. Create, position, and size your line normally.

2. Double-click the line to bring up the Edit Graphics Line dialog box.

3. Choose a different look for your line by clicking the Line Style button. A palette of different line patterns appears.

4. Click a pattern that appeals to you; an example of your line appears in the dialog box just to the left of the OK button.

   If you decide you don't want to use that kind of line style after all, click the **Line Style** button again and choose a different look.

5. Choose OK after you've picked a look for your line.

"I HATE THIS!"

How do I get rid of this ugly thing?

When you first experiment with lines, you'll probably make some mistakes and want to start over. You can get rid of your mangled line. Just click the line with your mouse to select it, and press Delete.

CHAPTER 16

Using Graphics in Your Documents

(Pretty as a Picture)

IN A NUTSHELL

▼ Insert a graphic into your
document
▼ Move the graphic to
a different place on
the page
▼ Change the size of
the graphic
▼ Customize the graphic
▼ Get rid of graphics you
don't want
▼ Make your own
graphics

his chapter shows you how to add pictures (called *graphics* and *clip art* in computer lingo) to your document. You can add a flag to your Race Day party invitation. Or add a trophy to your bowling league newsletter. Friends and enemies alike will be in awe of your computer prowess.

Graphics can add punch and pizzazz to your WordPerfect documents.

HOWLIN' WITH LONELINESS?

Call *Coyote Computer Dates* Now!

It's a bright, full moon, just made for romance, and you have nobody to howl at it with.

It doesn't *have* to be that way. *Coyote Computer Dates* can find you someone to be with. We guarantee it!

Here's how the program works. You send us your name, phone number, and $500.00. That's all you have to do—no questionnaires, no videotaped interviews, no psychological profiles to find out if you really belong in an institution. We then match you with someone else who has sent us his or her name, phone number, and $500.00. You'll have a date in no time!

Don't worry about whether you have anything in *common* with this person. We're sure you do. After all, you're both willing to give complete strangers $500 to match you up, at random, with yet another stranger, aren't you? Isn't that enough?

Do it today! Call (800) 555-DATE

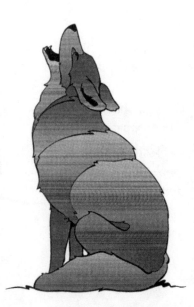

Graphics is a topic unto itself. This chapter is only a snapshot. For everything you care to know about graphics (and a whole lot more), consider picking up another Que book, *Using WordPerfect 6 for Windows*, Special Edition.

Can I Insert a Drawing of My Dog?

WordPerfect comes with a drawing tool (explained later in this chapter), so that you can theoretically draw anything you want and put it into WordPerfect. The truth is, however, it's very difficult for normal non-artistically gifted people to create any kind of drawing they would want in their documents. Even artistically minded folk have a tough time drawing things in computer programs—the mouse just doesn't make a great paintbrush.

What to do then? Use prefab graphics. These graphics are stored in a file on disk. Quite a few come with WordPerfect. If you want more, more, more, most computer stores sell packages of graphics files (called *clip art*) on a wide range of topics.

BUZZWORDS

CLIP ART

Clip art is any drawing or picture saved in a computerized format. You can add clip art to documents to snazz up the documents.

TIP

If you purchase a clip art package, be sure that the graphics format is compatible with WordPerfect (almost all are). Also, be aware that the quality of clip art images can vary from really outrageously good to very poor. Ask the salesperson to show you some samples from the package, preferably printed from WordPerfect.

If you buy clip art, don't be bamboozled by exciting colors in the graphics (unless you're one of the wealthy few with a color printer). All those colors may actually look *worse* when you print the graphic and WordPerfect tries to guess what shade of gray should correspond to your colors. High-contrast black-and-white graphics look best on the printed page.

Using Graphics in Documents (A picture is worth...)

There are lots of options for graphics. Do you want to mess with most of them? Heck no. Just follow these steps to plop graphics into your document; then read the next section on how to move and size them to be just right.

1. Decide what graphics file you want to use.

Graphics files have file names, just like documents do. You can see what graphics are available by looking at the "Graphic Images" appendix in your WordPerfect manual. The name of the file is under the picture of the graphic. Make a note of the graphics file name you want to use. If you can't find the manual, you can find a good graphic by trial and error.

2. Move the insertion point so that it's somewhere in the page you want the graphic.

3. Choose **Graphics**, **Figure**. Or, if you have the Button Bar handy, click the Figure button.

The Insert Image dialog box comes up, in which you type the name of the graphic you want to use.

4. If you know the name of the file, type it in the Filename text box and choose OK.

If you don't know the name of the file, scroll through the list box until you've found the file you want; then double-click it.

TIP

If you see a graphics file name but don't know what the graphic looks like, there's a way you can look at the graphic before you use it. Highlight the file you want to preview and choose View. The graphic image appears on-screen. You can then either choose Cancel to return to the document window, click another graphics file to preview it, or put the graphic in your document by choosing OK.

On-screen, in the upper right corner, you see the graphic. Ooooh. Aaaaah.

Checklist

✔ WordPerfect automatically wraps text around graphics. You don't have to worry about your document writing over the top of a graphic.

continues

241

I HATE WORDPERFECT FOR WINDOWS!

✔ You can do much more with the graphic: change its size, change its placement on the page, and on and on. Try experimenting. Or get a bigger, fatter, more expensive book on WordPerfect—for instance, *Using WordPerfect 6 for Windows*, Special Edition, published by Que. (Say—Que also published the book you're reading now. What a coincidence.)

✔ Graphics look their best when you print them at high resolution. When you want to print a document that contains graphics, choose **File**, **Print**. At the Print dialog box, click and hold the Print Quality pop-up menu button, and then choose **High**. You can then continue printing as you normally do.

✔ If you get a `This file does not exist` message when you type the name in step 4, choose OK and try typing the name again. Be sure that you type it correctly. If you get the same message a second time, scroll through the list box and double-click the file instead.

✔ Even though the graphics are in color on-screen, they won't be in color on your printed page—unless you're one of the few lucky stiffs who has a color printer, in which case you have permission to feel smug, knowing that I am jealous of you.

Moving and Sizing Graphics

By default, WordPerfect puts your graphic in the upper right corner of the page. That's fine, sometimes, but you may want to move the graphic to a different part of the page. To do it, move the mouse pointer so that the tip of it is on the graphic, click the mouse button, drag the graphic to where you want it, and then let go of the mouse button. That's all.

You might want to make the graphic bigger or smaller. With a mouse, it's a snap. Here's how:

1. Click on the graphic to select it.

The graphic has little black squares—called *handles*—and a box around it.

2. Click—and hold down the mouse button—on one of the corner handles; then drag the graphic until it's the size you want.

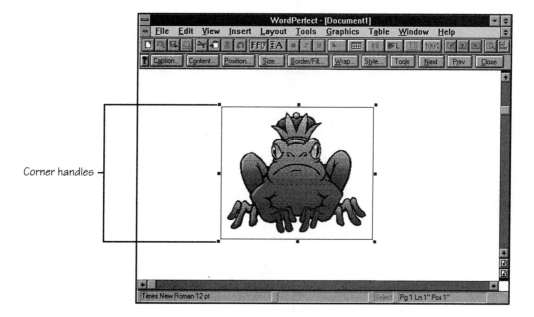

Corner handles

Click on the corner you want to move. For example, if you click on the bottom left corner, you size the graphic by moving that corner—the upper right corner stays where it is.

3. Release the mouse button.

The graphic appears in its new size.

TIP

It's good to be able to see the whole page when you're working with graphics—especially when you're moving the graphic. Click the Power Bar's Full Page Zoom button to see the whole page while you're working with the graphic; then click it again to go back to your original view.

Customizing the Graphic (Stupid graphics tricks)

After you've got the graphic the size and place you want it, you're usually done with it. Occasionally, though, you may be in the mood to impress your boss and amaze your coworkers. It's graphic-customizing time.

When you want to customize your graphic, first click the graphic to select it. Next, choose Graphics, Edit Box to bring up the Graphics Feature bar. Finally, use the Graphics Feature bar in the following tips to tweak your graphic to perfection.

EXPERTS ONLY

Flowin' or contourin' text

Usually, text beside the graphic automatically wraps to the next line whenever it gets close to the edge of the graphic. You can, however, have text flow right across the graphic or contour around the graphic itself.

Choose the feature bar's Wrap button to bring up the Wrap Text dialog box. Next, choose one of the radio buttons in the Wrapping Type group box. Choose Contour if you want your text to go to the edge of the graphic before it wraps to the next line. (If you use this option, your graphic shouldn't have

a border—see the following checklist item to learn how to remove it.) Choose N**o** Wrap if you want the text to go right through the graphic (which usually looks awful). Choose Neither side if you want text to stay above and below the graphic—never beside it. And finally, choose **S**quare to have the text go to the border of the graphic, and then wrap.

Tips for fancy graphics

✔ You don't have to stick with that plain-Jane single border around your graphic. You can have any number of fancy graphics—or none at all. Click the feature bar's **B**order/Fill button to bring up the Box Border/Fill Styles dialog box. Click the big square button next to **B**order Style to see a palette of borders you can have around your graphic. Click the one you want or, if you don't want a border at all, click the NO BORDER square. Choose OK.

✔ You can give your graphics captions, just like in a magazine (or like some of the graphics in this book). Click the feature bar's **C**aption button to bring up the dismayingly huge Box Caption dialog box. Don't panic; you don't have to do anything in this box but choose **E**dit. The dialog box disappears, and the insertion point appears below the graphic, beside a number (that is the number of your graphic). You can press Backspace to get rid of the number, if you want; then type your caption. When you're done typing the caption, just click anywhere in the document.

✔ When you're finished with the Graphics feature bar, just click the feature bar's **C**lose button.

Removing the Graphic (No pictures, please)

You might change your mind and decide that you don't need that picture of a tiger's head at the top of your Master's thesis after all. It's easy to get rid of the graphic. Just click it, and then press Delete.

Making Your Own Drawings in WordPerfect (For the Michelangelo in you)

WordPerfect lets you make your own drawings to put in the program, like this:

Author's lame attempt at drawing something in WordPerfect.

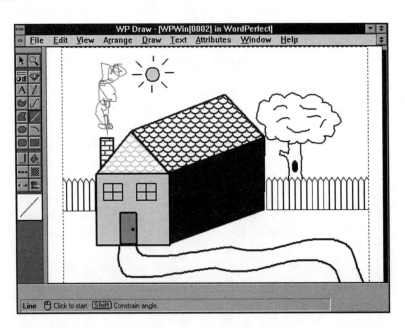

"I HATE THIS!"

My drawing looks like it was done by a four-year old!

Don't feel bad if you aren't able to draw any Picasso-quality works of art, either. It's just plain hard to draw with a mouse.

To start drawing something in WordPerfect, make sure that your insertion point is in the page where you want the drawing; then choose **G**raphics, **D**raw. Or, if you have the Button Bar showing, just click the Draw button.

The WP Draw window appears, and you can begin your drawing. You can draw freehand, as well as make straight lines and shapes. Just click the Tool Palette's drawing tool you want to use, and then do your thing. The tools are explained in the following checklist.

After you've finished your drawing, choose **F**ile, **C**lose and Return to Document. A box appears, asking if you want to save your changes. Choose **Y**es. Your drawing appears in the document window, where you can now size, move, and otherwise customize it like you would any graphic.

Drawing tools of the trade

✔ **Pointer:** This tool lets you select items you've already drawn so that you can drag them to new positions, modify them (by changing their colors or borders), or just plain delete them (by pressing Delete). You can select more than one thing by clicking and dragging over the area for everything you want to select.

✔ **Zoom:** When you click this tool, two more buttons appear—one is a magnifying glass with a + in it. Click this tool, and then click and drag over an area you want to see close up. When you're done with the close-up view, click the Zoom tool again and click the Full-Size button (the tool beside the magnifying glass with a + in it) to see the whole picture again.

continues

✔ **Insert Chart:** This tool is for placing a graph or chart inside a drawing you are making. It's awfully complex—avoid it.

✔ **Insert Figure:** Believe it or not, you can have a graphic *inside* the drawing you are making. Click this tool, and move the mouse pointer to where you want the upper left corner of the graphic to be inserted. Click and drag to where the lower right corner of the graphic should go. When you release the mouse button, the Retrieve Figure dialog box appears. Double-click the graphic you want to be inside your drawing.

✔ **Add Text:** Use this tool when you want text as part of your drawing. Click this tool, move the mouse pointer to where you want the text. Click the mouse, and then begin typing. You can also change the font by choosing **Text**, **Font**, and then—in the Font dialog box—choosing a font and size you want. Click outside the box when you are finished typing.

✔ **Freehand:** This tool is good for when you just want to draw normally—not using straight lines, specific shapes, or funky curves. Click this tool, move the pointer to where you want to start drawing, and then click and hold the mouse button while you start drawing. The pencil is on the paper whenever you have the mouse button pressed down.

✔ **Closed Curve:** This is a very tricky tool to use—it makes curvy shapes, and some pretty strange ones, at that. After clicking this tool, click where you want the shape to begin. Next, click at the peak of what will be the curve. Keep clicking in various places—each click is the peak of a curve. When you finally double-click, that closes off the shape, so the place where you double-click is connected to the beginning point of the shape.

✔ **Curve:** This tool works like the closed curve, except it just makes a curvy line, not a closed-off shape. When you double-click at the end of making this curvy line, it just ends the line. I can't make anything real-looking with this tool, either.

✔ **Polygon:** Ahhh, finally a tool that's easy to use. You can use it to make a shape with as many sides as you want. Click this tool, and then click where you want the shape to begin. Move the mouse pointer and click wherever you want to add a corner to the shape. When you're done with the shape, double-click. WordPerfect will connect your end-point with the beginning point. If you want to keep your lines so that they're only horizontal, vertical, or at 45 degrees, hold down the Shift key while you do all this.

✔ **Line:** You say you can't even draw a straight line? With this tool you can. Click this tool. Move the pointer to where you want the line to begin, click, move to where you want the line to end, and double-click. Or, if you want to continue the line in a dot-to-dot fashion, just click again to make a corner in the line. You can keep clicking corners in the line as long as you want. When you're done, double-click to end the line. If you want to keep your lines so that they're only horizontal, vertical, or at 45 degrees, hold down the Shift key while you do all this.

✔ **Oval:** Click this tool to make all kinds of circles and round shapes. Click at the highest, leftmost point for the round shape, and then drag the mouse pointer down and to the right until the shape looks the right size. If you want the shape to be a perfect circle, hold down the Shift key while you do this.

✔ **Elliptical Arc:** Click this tool if you want to make an arc, which is a segment of an oval or circle. Click where you want the arc to begin, and then click where you want the arc to end. If you want the arc to be like a segment from a circle, hold down the Shift key while you do this. If you want the arc to arc in the opposite direction, hold down the Alt key while you do this.

continues

✔ **Rounded Rectangle:** Click this tool to create a rectangle with rounded corners. Click where you want the upper left corner, and then drag to where you want the lower right corner. Hold down the Shift key while you do this if you want it to be a square.

✔ **Rectangle:** Click this tool when you want to make a regular rectangle. Click where you want the upper left corner, and then drag to where you want the lower right corner. Hold down the Shift key while you do this if you want it to be a square.

✔ **Border On/Off:** The Closed Curve, Polygon, Oval, Rounded Rectangle, and Rectangle tools all have two parts: the *border*, which is the outside edge of the shape, and the *fill*, which is the color inside the shape. Click this tool if you want to turn off the border on the shapes you create next, or to get rid of the border of the selected shape. Click this tool again to reverse the process.

✔ **Fill On/Off:** The fill is the color and pattern inside a shape. Click this tool to not have any color and pattern in the shapes you create next (or in the selected shape). Click the tool again to reverse the process.

✔ **Line Thickness:** You don't have to stick with a pencil-thin line or border in your drawings. Click this tool to get a palette of alternate thicknesses. Click the thickness you want.

✔ **Fill Pattern:** By default, your shapes are filled with a solid color. You can, however, fill them with a pattern. Click this tool, and then select a pattern from the palette that pops up.

✔ **Line Color:** Your lines and borders don't have to be black—they can be whatever color you fancy. Click this tool, and then choose a color from the dazzling display that appears before you.

✔ **Fill Color:** Choose whatever color you like for the color that fills your shapes. Click this tool, and then click the color you want to use. Keep in mind that unless you have a color printer, this is all going to come out in black and shades of gray (boy, I'll bet that rained on your parade).

TIP

Besides making your own drawings, you can use WordPerfect's Drawing feature to change and customize existing drawings. Just bring the graphic you want into your document, and then double-click it to bring it into the Draw part of the program. From there, just treat it like you drew it yourself. You can draw whatever you want on top of the existing graphic.

CHAPTER 17

Using Columns
(Your Own Newspaper)

IN A NUTSHELL

- ▼ Set up margins to give your columns extra space
- ▼ Place a headline above columns
- ▼ Create columns
- ▼ Put borders between columns
- ▼ Typing text into columns
- ▼ Make pull-quotes to go between columns

You might get so good at WordPerfect that you'll want to set up your own press. You could publish a family newsletter, detailing how the burglary charges against Little Jimmy were dropped and how much happier Pop has been since he got those new dentures. You might set up a neighborhood newsletter, or a company newsletter, or a newsletter for cat haters. Anything you want.

You *could* lay out your newsletter with one plain column, but you'd be announcing to your family, neighbors, and coworkers that you're an amateur. Instead, use two or three columns and impress your subscribers. Take a look at the document on the next page. It has two columns and a cool pull-quote in the center of the page; these funky elements pique the interest of your subscribers and make them want to read more.

You can use columns for anything you want, of course, but the most common reason people venture into the world of columns is to create a newsletter.

Before You Begin

You're ready to type your first story about Uncle Dale and Aunt Dot's vacation in Dollywood. But wait. First, you have to ask a few questions: What kind of margins do you want around the page? Do you want a headline above the columns? How about a header with the name of the newsletter and the page number at the top of each page? You should consider these issues before you start creating columns.

Columns make your
newsletters look
extraordinary

NEWS FROM THE BRADYS

Volume III, Issue 2   May 12, 1968

WELCOME . . .
To another edition of "News From The Bradys," the newsletter we send to all our friends and family to keep you in touch with what our ultra-normal family is doing.

NEWS IN THE NEIGHBORHOOD
Before we get started with each of the kids' antics (and believe me, they've been busy this month), I thought I'd respond to all the letters I've recently received asking about that pesky Partridge family that lives down the street.

Yes, they still practice until all hours of the night. Nobody can sleep. June Cleaver, our next door neighbor, has been especially affected by that nasty Danny Partridge's incessant drumming. She's so upset she can't eat and her hands shake. I could tell how bad she's taking all this noise when the other day I heard her shout, "Darn it Ward, how could you have *ever* come up with such a stupid name as "Beaver?!" I wouldn't be surprised if June has to make another trip to the psychiatrist before too long.

Back to the Partridges, though. No, they still haven't painted that horrible bus. No, Ms. Partridge still hasn't found a respectable husband, And finally, yes, they still have that Reuben Kincaid character as their manager (maybe *he's* her love interest, perish the thought). It seems that every time he finds them a gig, it winds up being in a haunted cave, a federal prison or who knows where else. Beggars can't be choosers, I suppose.

> ## "I've seen Marsha more than once with that nasty Laverne and Shirley. Imagine my humiliation."

ONE OTHER NOTE
I keep getting letters from some rather nasty relatives and even a few complete strangers wondering about my past. For those of you who are wondering who my first husband was, it's none of your business.

ABOUT ALICE
What would a Brady Newsletter be without a little bit about everybody's favorite housekeeper, maid, cook, and auto mechanic? Yes, of course I mean our very own Alice.

I recently got a call from Richie (you know, the Cunningham boy just across town who looks so much like his younger brother, Opie). He was wondering whether Alice has a last name.

Of course, I put the question directly to Alice and she responded, "Not as far as I know. I'm just here because I make good sandwiches and do a great job of making silly remarks, thereby setting the rest of you up for snappy comebacks." Hmmm. Alice seems a little bitter today.

MARSHA MADNESS
Now, onto our children. This issue, we'll start at the oldest—Marsha—and work down. Although now that I think about it, Greg may actually be our oldest. I can never be sure.

One thing that's been concerning me lately is the company Marsha tends to keep. I've seen her more than once with that nasty Laverne and Shirley. Imagine my

Making Small Margins

First, it's a good idea to use smaller margins for a document with several columns than you would for a document with only one column. With the regular one-inch margins, you wouldn't have much space for the columns themselves. You'll want smaller page margins—probably one-half inch on all four sides.

This is how you change the margins:

1. Press Ctrl+Home to make sure that the insertion point is at the top of the document.

2. Choose Layout, Margins. The Margin dialog box appears.

3. Type 0.5 for the Left, Right, Top and Bottom margins. You can press Tab to move from one text box to the next.

4. Choose OK to return to the document screen.

Now you have half-inch margins all the way around, which gives you a lot more room for your columns. The art of changing margins is more fully discussed in Chapter 12.

Making a Headline (Read all about it!)

When you use columns, you usually want a headline or banner (like the name of the newsletter) above them. This is where you can put to work all your knowledge of formatting—making text bigger, bolder, and badder.

Here's how you make a headline:

1. Press Ctrl+Home to be certain that the insertion point is at the top of the document.

2. Choose Layout, Line, Center to turn on WordPerfect's Center feature.

3. Choose Layout, Font to go to the Font dialog box.

4. Choose a gigantic font for your headline (48 point or even larger), and then choose OK.

5. Type the name of your newsletter or your headline or the name of your master's thesis—whatever you want.

6. Choose Layout, Font and select the font you'll be using for the main text in the document.

7. Choose OK.

You can quit here if you like. Or you can add a *subtitle*. Here's how to make a subtitle:

1. Press Enter twice to move the insertion point below the title.

2. Type any information you want to appear below and to the left of the title—like the volume and issue number.

3. Choose Layout, Line, Flush Right to move the insertion point to the right edge of the page.

4. Choose Insert, Date, Date Text to insert the date.

Still want more? If you want to add a line, press Enter to move below the issue number and date. Choose Graphics, Horizontal Line. This puts a horizontal line at the bottom of your *banner* (the name and subheading of the newsletter). For a line on using lines, read Chapter 15.

Press Enter twice to put some distance between the banner and the body of the document.

Creating the Columns (Divvying up the page)

After you've taken care of setting up the margins and banner for your document, you're all set to go with the columns. Turning on the columns feature is the easiest part of using columns. Here's what to do:

1. Move the insertion point to where you want the columns to begin—generally after the banner or headline.

2. Move the mouse pointer to the Columns button on the Power Bar, and then press and hold down the mouse button.

A menu pops up showing the various numbers of columns you can use.

3. While still holding down the mouse button, highlight the number of columns you want to use by dragging the pointer down the menu.

If the document already contains text, that text jumps into columns. If not, just start typing; the text forms into columns as you type.

TIP

Don't use more than three or four columns. Otherwise, the columns start getting so narrow that each line can only hold one or two words.

Fancy Columns

If you want your columns to look truly fancy, you can put lines between the columns. No, not with a Bic ballpoint—with WordPerfect!

Here's how to jazz up your document with lines between columns:

1. First create the columns. If you forget how to create columns, flip back to the section "Creating the Columns" earlier in this chapter.

2. Choose Layout, Columns, Border/Fill. The Column Border dialog box appears.

3. Click the large, square button by Border Style in the dialog box.

A palette of border styles pops up, but you're only interested in one—the one the pointer is next to, shown here:

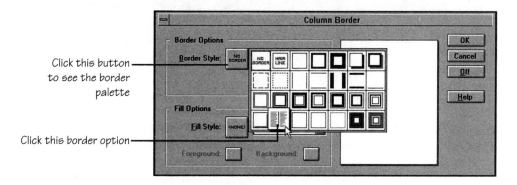

Click this button to see the border palette

Click this border option

4. Click the option shown in the figure.

5. Choose OK.

Now when you type text for the columns, lines appear between the columns. If you've already typed the text that you're putting into columns, the lines appear instantly.

Typing the Text

The final step in creating your newsletter is typing the text. Just type away. You can move, copy, delete, make bold, and do everything you can do in a "normal" (one-column) document. The only difference is how the text wraps. When you get to the bottom of one column, WordPerfect takes you to the top of the next one. When you get to the bottom of the last column on a page, WordPerfect takes you to the beginning of the first column on the next page.

Checklist

✔ If you are only part-way down a column, but you want to end that column and begin the next one, click and hold the Column button on the Power Bar. Then choose Column Break (or just press Ctrl+Enter). The insertion point jumps to the beginning of the next column.

✔ If you don't like the text in columns and long for the old one-column format, move your insertion point to where the columns begin. Click and hold the Column button on the Power Bar, and then choose Columns Off. The document goes back to the one-column look.

Can I Quote You on That? (Using pull-quotes in your newsletter)

If you're feeling adventurous and have a little time to kill, you might want to try putting a pull-quote in your newsletter, like the one in the sample newsletter at the beginning of this chapter. They take a little bit of work, but they make the newsletter look more interesting.

BUZZWORDS

PULL-QUOTE

A box with an interesting snippet of text from a magazine or newspaper article, set in big text in a prominent place. The idea behind a pull-quote is to get you interested in the article so that you'll read the whole thing—not just skim it in line at the grocery store. So, you wouldn't want to have a pull-quote that said something like, "Integration of the hyperpercolator has been repeatedly ignored by ambivalent office workers." Look for something snappy and easy to understand.

The first thing to do when you're going to make a pull-quote is find some juicy little phrase or sentence in the newsletter that will make the reader want to find out more. Select that text (keep it short—usually no more than a sentence), and then copy it to the Clipboard. (Choose Edit, Copy to copy text to the Clipboard.) Click anywhere on the page to deselect the text.

Now you're set to create the pull-quote. Choose Graphics, Text. Or, if you have the Button Bar showing, click on the Text Box button. Two horizontal bars appear in your document, with an insertion point between them. Choose Edit, Paste to paste the text into the document.

With the text in the pull-quote box, you just need to customize it so it stands out—you can do this by centering it and using a large font. Here's how:

1. Press Ctrl+Home to go to the beginning of the text in the pull-quote.

2. Choose **Layout, Justification, Center** to center the text. Now you're ready to change the font size.

3. Now choose **Layout, Font**. The Font dialog box appears.

4. In the Font dialog box, choose a font different from the one you're using in the rest of the newsletter. Then choose a large size for the font—say, 18 to 24 points. (If you want to know more about using fonts, flip back to Chapter 3.)

5. Choose OK. Voila!

If you want to edit the text in the pull-quote, that's just fine. Edit it like you would any text.

Once your text is just how you want it, you're set to move the pull-quote where you want it. This procedure is easier than you think. Just click on the pull-quote and drag it to where you want it—probably in the middle of the page, between a couple of columns. Any text in that part of the page automatically wraps around the pull-quote.

Pull-quote pointers

✔ You're not stuck with the size of the pull-quote. You can make it fatter or skinnier, longer or shorter, drier or fruitier. Just click on it so that handles appear, and then drag the handles so that the box is the size you want. (For a closer look at how to handle handles, see "Moving and Sizing Graphics" in Chapter 16.)

✔ If you change the size of the pull-quote, make sure that you don't make it so small the text won't fit. If you make the box too small, part of your pull-quote's text will be cut out.

✔ Don't use column borders and pull-quotes in the same area. The border line will print right through the pull quote—a tacky look at best.

✔ If you need to edit the text in an existing pull-quote, move the mouse pointer over the pull-quote, and then click the *right* mouse button. A menu appears. Choose Edit Text, and the insertion point appears inside the quote.

CHAPTER 18

Using Tables
(Setting the Table)

IN A NUTSHELL

- ▼ Create a table
- ▼ Change the column width
- ▼ Join cells
- ▼ Type text into a table
- ▼ Add columns and rows to a table
- ▼ Remove rows and columns from a table

reating a table without a special table feature is a nightmare. If you've ever typed a table, you know what I mean. You type the first column and tab to move to the second column. You type the text for that column, but uh-oh, one of the words in column 2 wraps to the next line. You can press Tab to move it in line with the second column, but what if you add text? Who knows where anything will line up? What if the second row is longer than the first? You'll have to readjust the second column again!

If you need to organize a lot of information so that it stays in order and is easy to find, it's time you got to know the Tables feature.

The Tables feature lets you quickly organize and categorize information.

Homes For Sale In My Price Range							
Address	Price	Sq. ft	# bedrm	# bath	# car gar.	A/C	Rating
974 W Bernard St	94,000	1480	3	2	2	Yes	***
8201 Hooligan Rd	88,900	1200	2	1.5	1	Yes	**
46 Townshend Circle	96,200	1360	3	2.5	2	Yes	**
232 Peach Street	102,000	1722	4	3	2	Yes	****

This chapter shows you how to make a table and how to make it look good.

Creating a Table

Before you dive into the Table feature, you need to do a little planning. First, the million-dollar question: How many columns and rows do you need? It's better to overestimate than underestimate, so be generous. If you find out later that you need more—or fewer—columns or rows, though, don't fret. You can change the number of rows and columns that your table contains.

BUZZWORDS

COLUMNS, ROWS, and CELLS

Tables are composed of rows, columns, and cells. A *column* goes up and down the page. A *row* goes across the page. A *cell* is where the columns and rows cross. A cell looks like a rectangle and is what you type a number or word into.

After you've figured out the number of columns and rows you need, you're ready to make the table. Here's what you do:

1. Move the insertion point to where in the document you want the table.

Make sure that you move the insertion point to the beginning of a blank line.

TIP

If your table will have more than four or five columns, set narrow left and right margins to make room for all those columns. You learn how to set margins in Chapter 12.

2. Click and hold on the Power Bar's Table button.

A grid appears, with No Table at the top.

3. Drag on the grid until you have highlighted the number of columns and rows you want.

As you drag the mouse pointer on the grid, the top of the grid reports how many columns and rows you have selected, like this: 5x7. The first number tells you how many columns are selected; the second number tells you how many rows are selected.

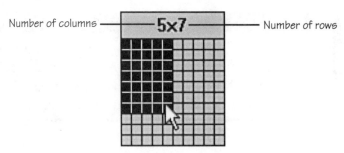

Number of columns ———— 5x7 ———— Number of rows

4. Release the mouse button.

The table appears, with the insertion point positioned inside, ready for you to do the tabular thing.

Checklist

✔ The largest table you can make with the Power Bar's Table button is 32 columns wide by 45 rows deep. That's a plenty big table for most folks, but you may want more. If so, move the insertion point to where you want the table, and choose Table, Create to open the Create Table dialog box. In the Columns box, type the number of columns you want; in the Rows box, type the number of rows you want. Then choose OK.

✔ No matter *how* you create the table, it can't have more than 64 columns (you can have a huge number of rows, however). Remember, all those columns have to fit between the left and right margins of the page, so the more columns you have, the less space you'll have in each column.

✔ If you've already made a table using tabs, you don't have to retype the whole thing. Instead, select everything in the tabular column, and then choose Table, Create, OK.

Slimfast or Steroids?
(Making columns thinner or wider)

When you first create a table, WordPerfect makes each of the columns the same width so that, together, they fill the space between the margins. It's likely, however, that you'll want some of the columns to be wider than others—so that the information will fit in the cell.

To change the width of a column, move the mouse pointer on top of the vertical line you want to move. When the mouse pointer is in just the right place, it changes to look like the pointer in the following figure.

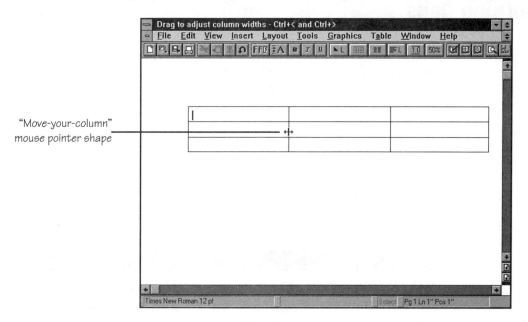

"Move-your-column" mouse pointer shape

When your pointer is this shape, click (and hold) the mouse button and drag the column left or right. When you release the mouse button, that edge of the column is moved to the next point.

CAUTION

You can only move a column edge so far. You can't move it past the edge of another column, and you can't move column edges on top of each other. Each column has to have a little space of its own.

Joining Cells

Your table will look classy if you use the first row for a table title, such as "Third-Quarter Sales Results" or "Pros and Cons of Rug Burns." To do this, you need to join all the cells in your first row into one giant cell you can type the table title into.

To join cells, click (and hold) the mouse button in the first cell you want joined, and then drag across to the last cell you want joined. Usually, this means dragging across the entire first row. Next, choose **T**able, **J**oin, **C**ell. Voila—one cell going across the entire table. You can now type the title.

Table title tips

✔ Once you've created a first row for your table, you'll probably want to format it so that it stands out. With the insertion point in that row, Choose Layout, Line, Center to center the title. You might also want to choose a large bold font. See Chapter 3 for a rundown on how to pick a font.

✔ If your table is going to go on for more than one page, you may want the title to appear at the top of each page. Choose Table, Format to bring up the Format dialog box; then choose the Row radio button. Now, at the bottom of the dialog box, select the Header Row check box. Choose OK to go back to the table. Your title will now be at the top of the table on each page. If the second row in your table is the name of each column, you might want to select the first two rows before following these steps; that way, both rows will be at the top of each page.

Typing Text into a Table

Now you're all set to type the information that goes in your table. To type text into the table, move to the cell where you want to add text; then just type the text. Press Tab to move from one cell to the next. To move backward, press Shift+Tab. If you want to move up and down, use the up- and down-arrow keys. If you're using a mouse to move the insertion point around, click in the cell you want to add text to.

Checklist

✔ If the text in one cell has to be more than one line high, WordPerfect automatically makes the row taller to fit any new lines of text.

✔ If you have very narrow columns in your table, you may not be able to fit a whole word or number on a single line, in which case WordPerfect wraps your text to a new line wherever it has to, like this:

continues

271

| ambi |
| dextr |
| ous |

To remedy this little *faux pas*, you can either make the column wider (see the section, "Slimfast or Steroids," earlier in this chapter), or you can abbreviate your text to keep it from wrapping in such an odd place.

✔ When you move the insertion point around in the table, the name of the cell shows up in the status bar. The columns are lettered—A, B, C, and so on—and are the first name of the cell. The rows are numbered—1, 2, 3, and so on—and are the last name of the cell. The cell name is made up of both the first and last name and looks like A1 or D27.

Adding Rows and Columns

It's hard to guess the exact number of rows and columns you'll want in a table. You always seem to have just one more item you have to put in the table.

To add extra rows or columns to your table, move the insertion point so that it's where you want to add the extra rows or columns. Choose Table, Insert. Choose the Columns or Rows radio button—whichever you want to add—and then, in the text box, type the number of rows or columns you want to add. Choose OK.

TIP

If you're in the last cell in a table and decide you need another row for more stuff, you don't have to go to any work at all to create that row. From the last cell in the table (the one in the lower right corner), press Tab. Another row magically appears in the table.

Checklist

✔ If you want to add more rows, choose the **R**ows radio button, and then type the number of rows you want to add. Next, choose the **B**efore radio button if you want the new rows to be above the row your insertion point is in, or choose **A**fter if you want the new rows to be below the row your insertion point is in. Choose OK to affirm this change and to see the new rows.

✔ If you want to add more columns, choose **C**olumns, and then type the number of columns you want to add. Choose **B**efore to add the new columns to the left of the column your insertion point is in, or choose **A**fter to add the columns to the right of the column your insertion point is in. Choose OK.

Removing Rows and Columns (One less row to hoe)

Let's say that you enjoy adding rows and columns so much that you go hog-wild and add a bunch more than you need. Now what? Are you stuck with the spares? No. Just remove them.

Move the insertion point so that it's at the beginning of the set of rows or columns you want to delete. For example, if you want to delete four blank rows—say, rows 19, 20, 21, and 22—you'd move the insertion point so that it's in the first of those four rows (row 19). If you want to delete three columns—D, E, and F—you would move the insertion point so that it's somewhere in the first of these three columns—column D.

When you're ready to delete those rows or columns, choose **Table**, **Delete**. The Delete dialog box appears. Choose the **Rows** or **Columns** radio button, depending on which one you want to get rid of. Next, type how many rows you want to delete; then choose OK and those unwanted cells just disappear!

CAUTION

You can only use the preceding method to delete multiple rows or columns if they're next to each other. If there are rows or columns between the ones you want to delete (for example, if you want to delete rows 19, 27, 30, and 33), you cannot use this method.

CAUTION

Make sure that the rows or columns are either blank or contain text that you don't want. When you delete a row, any text in that row is also deleted.

TIP

If you delete more than you bargained for, you can bring them back, but only if you act quickly. Choose **Edit**, **Undo** immediately.

CHAPTER 19

Speeding Things Up with Macros

(The Not-So-Scary World of Macros)

IN A NUTSHELL

▼ Learn what a macro is

▼ Make macros

▼ Fix a macro you recorded incorrectly

▼ Use macros

▼ Put your address in a document

▼ Turn on page numbering

▼ Create a footer with the document's file name in it

Macros. The word strikes fear into the heart of almost all WordPerfect users. And why not? *Macro* sounds like something a mad scientist might name his pet robot.

But when you get to know them, macros aren't scary at all. In fact, a *macro* is just a shortcut. For example, if you write a lot of letters, you might like to have a shortcut for typing your address. This chapter shows you how to make a macro that types your entire address when you press a keystroke combination. You also learn about several other macro shortcuts that make using WordPerfect easier.

Making and Using Macros

Creating WordPerfect macros is like making audio tapes on a tape recorder. When you want to record something on a tape recorder, you follow certain steps. First, you pop a tape into the machine. Next, you press the Record button. You say what you need to say, and then you turn off the tape recorder.

Later, when you want to play back what you said, you find the tape and put it back in the machine. Then you press Play. You don't have to do anything else—just let the tape recorder do the talking.

WordPerfect macros work the same way. Instead of recording your voice, however, they record and play back actions you perform in WordPerfect.

To make a macro, you first name the macro with a keystroke combination like Ctrl+Shift+X—this is like popping a tape into the tape recorder and pressing Record. Next, you do the steps you want in the macro shortcut. For example, if you want a macro to turn on Print Preview, you press the keystrokes to turn on Print Preview. After you've done everything that you want to be part of the shortcut, you stop recording the macro.

Later, when you want WordPerfect to do those steps again, you just play the macro by pressing the same keystroke combination you used to name the macro. WordPerfect plays back the macro, doing all those steps for you—very quickly.

Recording a Macro (Record!)

TIP

Before you record a macro shortcut, go to a blank document window. That way, you won't put unwanted codes and text in the document you're using right now.

If you want to automate a task you perform over and over, create a macro. Here's how:

1. Choose Tools, Macro, Record.

This tells WordPerfect that you're about to create a macro.

The Record Macro dialog box appears, which is where you name the shortcut. What should you name the shortcut? Pick a letter. Almost any letter from A-Z will do.

TIP

Think of a letter that you can associate with the short-cut you're creating. For example, if you want a shortcut for typing your address, you can use A—for address.

2. Hold down the Ctrl and Shift keys and press the letter you want to use for this shortcut.

I HATE WORDPERFECT FOR WINDOWS!

In other words, press and hold down the Ctrl and Shift keys together. While still holding down those keys, press any letter. For example, you can press Ctrl+Shift+A if you want a shortcut for typing your address. Remember this keystroke combo so that you can use the shortcut later.

After you press the Ctrl+Shift+letter keystroke combo, ctrlsftx.wcm appears in the **N**ame text box. X is the letter you pressed.

TIP

All the good ones are taken

WordPerfect has already reserved a bunch of Ctrl+Shift+letter key combos for its own use. If you record a macro using those combos, you'll have problems when you try to use those shortcuts later. Namely, instead of playing the shortcut, WordPerfect will just do whatever it always has with that key combination. Here are the Ctrl+Shift+letter combinations you should avoid:

The Key Combo	What It Does
Ctrl+Shift+B	Puts a bullet in the document
Ctrl+Shift+D	Puts the date (as a code) in the document
Ctrl+Shift+O	Defines the Outline Style (whatever that means)
Ctrl+Shift+P	Puts the page number in the document
Ctrl+Shift+Q	Sets a QuickMark in the document
Ctrl+Shift+S	Saves all the open documents
Ctrl+Shift+Z	Undeletes the last text you erased

3. Choose **Record**.

`Macro Record` appears in the status bar at the bottom of the window.

You're all set to press the keys you want to be part of the shortcut.

4. Type the text or use the feature you want to be in the shortcut.

For example, if you wanted to make a macro that types your address, you would just type your address the same way you always would. If you wanted a macro that set page numbering in the upper right corner of the page, you would choose the menus and click the buttons you always would. As you work, WordPerfect records your actions.

"I HATE THIS!"

My mouse is messed up!

When you're recording a macro, there are certain things you can't do with a mouse. Mainly, you can't click in the document to move the insertion point—you need to use the arrow keys instead. If you are recording a macro and move the mouse somewhere to which WordPerfect takes offense, the mouse pointer appears as a circle with a slash through it. And clicking the mouse won't do anything. Not a thing.

5. Choose **Tools**, **Macro**, **Record** to stop recording the macro.

You're done.

I HATE WORDPERFECT FOR WINDOWS!

Checklist

✔ The shortcut for choosing **T**ools, **M**acro, **R**ecord is pressing the handy keystroke combo Ctrl+F10. Ditto goes for stopping the recording when you're done.

✔ You can type text for your macros or turn features on and off, or any combination of the two. Anything you do often in WordPerfect, you can do faster with a macro.

✔ You might want your macro to take you to a certain part of WordPerfect—such as the header editing window—and leave you there. That's fine. Just begin recording the macro and follow the steps you normally would to take you to the window you want. After you're there, choose **T**ools, **M**acro, **R**ecord to tell WordPerfect to stop recording. You can then leave the editing window normally.

✔ When you're recording a macro shortcut, don't rush through things! WordPerfect records your mistakes as well as everything else you do. Take your time. Do everything slowly and surely.

✔ When you choose **R**ecord to start recording a macro in step 3, you may see a prompt that says the macro already exists. This means you already have a macro by that name. Choose **N**o to cancel re-cording the macro (unless you *want* to replace the existing macro); then press a different Ctrl+Shift+letter combo.

✔ Besides naming your macros with Ctrl+Shift+letter combinations, you can also use just Ctrl+letter combinations—but I wouldn't recommend it. Why not? Most of the Ctrl+letter combinations on the keyboard are already reserved by WordPerfect! In fact, the only letters you can use in combination with Ctrl are F, H, M, and Y.

EXPERTS ONLY

Opening up a dialog

Hey, how about if you want to make a macro that brings up a dialog box, stops while you choose your options, then continues on its merry way? It could happen—say you want a macro that types some stuff, pauses while you change to a new font, and then types some more stuff.

Here's what you do. Record the macro like you usually do. When you come to the dialog box that you want the macro to pause on, however, look for a little check box in the upper right corner of the dialog box—up in the title bar. Choose the check box, and then choose OK or Close to close the dialog box.

Now, when you use this macro shortcut, the macro will pop up this dialog box and let you make whatever changes you need to. When you close the dialog box (by choosing OK, Close, Cancel, or whatever), the macro continues on its way.

Redoing the Macro (I goofed up!)

If you get lost or confused while creating a macro, choose **T**ools, **M**acro, and then choose **R**ecord to quit. Clear the screen, and then start over.

To record the macro again, choose **T**ools, **M**acro, **R**ecord. In the Record Macro dialog box, press the Ctrl+Shift+letter combo for the macro to be redone, and then choose **R**ecord. A prompt appears, telling you the macro already exists. Choose Yes. Now you can record the macro again. When you finish, choose **T**ools, **M**acro, **R**ecord to stop recording.

Using Your Macro Shortcuts (Play!)

After you create the macro shortcut, all the hard work is done. Now you can save time by using the macro shortcut.

Move the insertion point to where you want it to be when you play back the macro.

If you're about to use a macro shortcut that types your address, for example, you would move the insertion point to where you want to insert your address.

Press the Ctrl+Shift+letter keystroke combo used to name the macro when you created it.

That's it. The macro goes to work, often finishing its task before you can blink.

"I HATE THIS!"

My macro doesn't work on Wallace's machine!

Your macro shortcuts only work on your machine. If you try them on another person's copy of WordPerfect, nothing will happen. You'll have to create the macro on the other machine as you did on yours.

Macros You Can Use

There are certain WordPerfect tasks most users do over and over again. This section shows you the steps to create macro shortcuts for some of these common WordPerfect tasks. These are just ideas, though; feel free to experiment and create your own macros.

These steps are pretty bare bones; they don't detail what the prompts mean or what unexpected messages can pop up. You can learn more about recording and using macros at the beginning of this chapter.

Making an Address Macro

It's amazing how often you need to type your address: in letters, reports, anonymous threats—just about everything you write that requires a response of some sort. You can save the time it takes to type the address by making it a macro. You just start recording the macro, type your address the way you always do, and then stop recording the macro.

Here are the steps:

1. Choose **T**ools, **M**acro, **R**ecord.

2. Press Ctrl+Shift+A; then choose OK.

I chose Ctrl+Shift+A because A reminds me of **A**ddress. If you want to use a different letter keystroke combo, press that combination.

3. Type your address.

You can press Enter at the end of each line as part of your address. If you need your phone and fax number as part of your address, type that here, too.

4. Choose **T**ools, **M**acro, **R**ecord.

WordPerfect stops recording the macro shortcut.

✔ Whenever you want to put your address in a document, move the insertion point so that it's where you want the address to begin and press Ctrl+Shift+A. Your address appears almost instantly.

✔ You can use this same technique to make macro shortcuts for other text you use frequently. For example, you might want to make a Ctrl+Shift+N macro that inserts your name. You could make a Ctrl+Shift+C macro to insert the name of a college course you're taking (to go at the top of all those papers you have to write). There are probably other words or phrases you use often enough that you could save time by having a macro type them for you.

Turning on Page Numbering

You need page numbering in just about everything you write, so you'll probably use this macro—which adds page numbers to the upper right corner of the page—in just about every document. (You can make a slight adjustment and insert the number somewhere else on the page.)

Follow these steps:

1. Choose Tools, Macro, Record.

2. Press Ctrl+Shift+N; then choose Record.

The N stands for Page Numbering. (I would have used Ctrl+Shift+P, but it's already taken, darn the luck.)

Now you're ready to work your way through the menus to turn on page numbering.

3. Choose Layout, Page, Numbering.

The Page Numbering dialog box appears.

4. Click and hold the **P**osition pop-up menu (it looks like a wide button and probably contains the words `No Page Numbering`), and then drag to the type of page numbering you want, such as Top **R**ight. When you've got the right page numbering type high-lighted, let go of the mouse button.

5. Choose OK. You return to the document window.

6. Choose **T**ools, **M**acro, **R**ecord.

WordPerfect stops recording your macro shortcut.

Checklist

✔ If you want the page number to go somewhere else than the top right corner of the screen, choose a different option in step 4.

✔ When you want to use this macro, move the insertion point so that it's anywhere on the page where you want numbering to begin. Press Ctrl+Shift+N to start the macro.

Putting the Document Name in a Footer

Hmmm, now what was the file name of this special investigative report I've been working on? Was it DIEBARNY.WPD or KILBARNY.WPD? Or was it BARNYDOA.WPD? It's tough to remember file names, be-cause you've got just eight letters to work with. This macro can help. It puts the name of the document in a footer. That way, if you're looking at a printed copy of the document and see changes that should be made, you know the name of the document right away.

This is how you make the file-name-in-a-footer macro:

1. Choose **T**ools, **M**acro, **R**ecord.

2. Press Ctrl+Shift+F; then choose **R**ecord.

The F stands for **F**ile name. Or maybe it stands for **F**ooter. I'll let you decide.

3. Press Ctrl+Home to go to the top of the document; then choose **L**ayout, **H**eader/Footer to go to the Headers/Footers dialog box.

4. Choose the **F**ooter A radio button, and then choose **C**reate.

Now you're in the Footer editing window, in which you can enter the document's file name.

5. Choose **G**raphics, **H**orizontal Line to make a line that separates the footer from the rest of the document. Press Enter to go to the next line.

6. Choose **I**nsert, **O**ther, **F**ilename.

If you want to have the whole path (the drive and directory your file is in), you can choose **P**ath and Filename instead of just **F**ilename.

If your document has a file name, it appears here. If your document doesn't have a file name, nothing appears until you name the document.

7. Choose **F**ile, **C**lose to return to the document window, or choose the Feature Bar's Close button.

8. Choose **T**ools, **M**acro, **R**ecord.

WordPerfect stops recording your macro shortcut.

Now you can put a footer with the document's name into any document—just press Ctrl+Shift+F.

TIP

You might want the footer to appear in a different font than the body of the document. In that case, after step 5, choose **L**ayout, **F**ont, and then select a different font and size. (Most people have the font size smaller than the text in the rest of the document.) Choose OK to close the Font dialog box, and then continue with step 6.

PART V

The Quick and Dirty Dozens

Includes:

12 Cool Things You Can Do in WordPerfect

12 Major Don'ts When Using WordPerfect

12 Heart-Stopping WordPerfect Messages and What to Do about Them

12 Features You Should Leave Alone unless You Have Time to Kill

12 Common Problems

12 Best WordPerfect Shortcuts

I HATE

The Quick and Dirty Dozens

INCLUDES:

12 Cool Things You Can Do in WordPerfect

12 Major Don'ts When Using WordPerfect

12 Heart-Stopping WordPerfect Messages and What to Do about Them

12 Features You Should Leave Alone unless You Have Time to Kill

12 Common Problems

12 Best WordPerfect Shortcuts

12 Cool Things You Can Do in WordPerfect

1. Quick-Change Margins.

If you change your margins frequently, keep the Ruler handy.
(Choose **View**, **R**uler Bar to turn on the Ruler.) The left and right
margin markers are shown at the top of the Ruler. When you want
to change a left or right margin, move the insertion point to where
you want the change, click the margin marker, and drag it to its
new spot.

If you want to change all the margins or want to be very precise in
your margin changes, you can use the Ruler to bring up the Margin
dialog box. Double-click anywhere at the very top part of the Ruler
to bring up the Margins dialog box. Type in the measurements you
want for your margins, and then choose OK.

2. Automatic Tabbing.

One of the most common ways to show that you're beginning a
new paragraph is to indent the first line of that paragraph. Usually,
this means that you need to press Tab at the beginning of the
line. If you're feeling extra lazy (or extra efficient), you can set
WordPerfect to automatically indent the first line of your paragraphs. Move the insertion point so that it's where you want this
auto-indenting to begin (after the title, addresses, and date, usually). Choose Layout, **P**aragraph, **F**ormat to see the Paragraph Format dialog box. In the **F**irst Line Indent box, set the distance you
want to have the first line of each paragraph indented—**.3** is a
good amount—and then choose OK.

3. Pack Rat Saving.

If you're one of those amazing people who's able to think of three
or four things at a time, you'll probably start working on several

documents at once. No doubt you're also the conscientious type, so you want to keep all of your documents saved. Does this mean that every so often you ought to move from one document to another, saving as you go? No, that would be far too much work. Instead, when you want to save every document you have open, press Ctrl+Shift+S.

CAUTION

Don't use this trick unless you've already named each of your documents. Otherwise, the Save As dialog box pops up for each of the documents so that you can name them—but the dialog box doesn't tell you which document you're saving. Very confusing.

4. **Put foreign characters in your documents.**

Even if you don't speak another language, from time to time you'll probably need to put a foreign word in your documents—and that almost always means putting in some funky character with a tilde (~) or accent mark (´) over it. Choose Insert, **C**haracter (or press Ctrl+W) to see the WordPerfect Characters dialog box. Click the pop-up menu button in the Character **S**et group box, and then select the type of character you want to insert. For example, if you want to put a Spanish letter in your document, choose Multinational. A list of characters appears in the box. Scroll through the box until you find the character you want, and then choose Insert and Close.

Besides just foreign characters, you can find all kinds of bizarre symbols in the WordPerfect Characters dialog box. Try looking at the characters available in different character sets.

5. Words, words, words.

How much have you written today? If you're in the mood for a productivity check—or you get paid by the word—you can use WordPerfect to tell you how many words are in your document. Choose **File, Document Info**. The Document Information box appears, and the second line tells you how many words are in your document. The box also reports on how many characters you have, the average length of your sentence, the number of sentences, and several other things you probably don't need to know.

6. Save it for someone else.

It's a sad fact that not everybody uses WordPerfect for Windows. If you save your document on a floppy disk and give it to another person, he may not be able to open it. If you know what word processor that person uses, however, you can be a real friend and convert it to a format his computer can read. With your document already open and saved, choose **File, Save As**. Click the Format box at the bottom of the dialog box to see a list of word processing formats you can save in. Scroll through the list until you see the format you need, and then click it.

Now, in the Filename text box, type a different name for the document. (You can type the path name, too—for example you might type **A:YUCK** if you want to save the document with the file name YUCK on drive A.) Choose OK to save the document, and then close the document window *without* saving changes (to avoid accidentally resaving the document in WordPerfect format).

7. Joined at the hip.

It doesn't work to have dates or proper names split across two lines by WordPerfect. You can avoid this problem by pressing Ctrl+space bar (instead of just the space bar) between words

that need to be kept on the same line. If I were Elvis Presley, for instance, (and do you really know for absolutely sure that I'm *not*?) and I were typing my name, I would type **Elvis**, Ctrl+space bar, and *then* type **Presley**. That way, both my first and last name would stay on the same line.

8. **Does anybody really know what time it is?**

One of the most important questions in the world is "How long 'til 5:00?" To help answer this question, WordPerfect lets you display the time and temperature in the status bar. (Okay, the temperature isn't really displayed—but the time is.) Move the mouse pointer so it's pointing on the status bar, but not on any of the parts that show something. (For example, you shouldn't be pointing at the font or position.) Double-click to bring up the Status Bar Preferences dialog box. Scroll down through the list box until you see Time (12 Hour). Click the check box; then uncheck the Select On/Off check box to make room for the time on your status bar. Choose OK to go back to the document. From now on, your status bar will display the time.

9. **Swinging from document to document.**

If you work with more than one document at a time, you'd probably like to be able to switch from one to the next without having to use the menus. Easy enough. Just press Ctrl+F6 to go forward one document, or press Ctrl+Shift+F6 to go back one document.

10. **Dashing dashes.**

An em dash is, simply enough, a dash about the width of an *m*. People use them when they're not sure what punctuation they *really* should be using. You'll notice them in this book—right here, for instance. When using typewriters, people fake em dashes by

pressing the hyphen key (-) twice. Now that we've got computers, you can use *real* em dashes, which look better. Just press Ctrl+W to bring up the WordPerfect Characters dialog box, press the dash (-) key twice, and then press Enter.

11. **From uppercase to lowercase and back again.**

Suppose that you forget to capitalize a word. Or that you capitalized a word you shouldn't have. Or maybe you'd like to go overboard and capitalize the whole thing. No problem; with WordPerfect, you don't have to retype the word to change its capitalization. Instead, move the insertion point so that it's anywhere in the word and press Ctrl+K. WordPerfect changes the capitalization to something different. If the capitalization still isn't right, press Ctrl+K again. You shouldn't have to press Ctrl+K more than two or three times before WordPerfect has the word capitalized just how you want it.

12. **Hide and seek.**

Editing can be a nerve-wracking experience. You've got a questionable paragraph all blocked and ready to be deleted when you suddenly have misgivings. Maybe it's not such a bad paragraph. Maybe you ought to leave it in. Nah, take it out. No, leave it in. *Take it out.* LEAVE IT IN!

There's no point in putting yourself through this kind of anguish. You can have it both ways by using the Hidden Text feature. You can hide text you're pretty sure you don't need, but make it reappear if it turns out you *do* want it.

To hide some text, first select the text you want to hide. Choose **L**ayout, **F**ont to see the Font dialog box, and then check the Hidden check box (it's in the Appearance group box). Choose OK.

The selected text disappears—but you can bring it back if you want to. To make hidden text reappear, choose View, Hidden Text and your questionable text magically reappears.

Once you've marked text as hidden, you can make it appear and disappear again at your every whim by choosing View, Hidden Text.

12 Major Don'ts When Using WordPerfect

1. Don't use spaces to indent paragraphs.

Don't use the space bar to indent the beginning of a paragraph or to make columns.

The space bar is a tempting key—it's so much bigger than all the others. You may be in the habit of pressing the space bar five times each time you start a new paragraph, or using the space bar to line up columns of information. Get out of the habit quickly. If you use the space bar to begin paragraphs or start columns, things probably won't line up on the printed page.

Use the Tab key instead. The Tab key was made specifically for beginning paragraphs.

2. I said don't use spaces!

Don't use the space bar to go to the next line in a document. When you need to put some space between paragraphs or lines in a document, don't lean on the space bar until you've created those lines of space. If you ever edit your work, those spaces will shift around and wreak havoc on your document. Instead, when you need to move down a line, just press Enter. If you need to move down a few lines, press Enter a few times. Don't, however, use Enter to go all the way to the next page (that's the next tip).

3. Don't use Enter to go to the next page.

Don't use the Enter key to go to the next page. If you've just finished a title page and want to begin on a fresh page for the body of your document, don't keep pressing Enter until you see that page break. Instead, just press Ctrl+Enter.

4. **Don't mess with the Preferences.**

WordPerfect is incredibly customizable. You can change what's on the menus, change what buttons are on the Power Bar, change what the status bar does and how it looks, and more, more, more. WordPerfect is a perfect example of the "plenty of rope to hang yourself" syndrome. The menus, bars, and other various thingamajigs in WordPerfect are where they are because they work well that way. Trust me on this.

5. **Don't go on a pell-mell replacing spree.**

Don't blindly replace one file with another. You've been typing away at a new document, and it's time to give it a name. You choose **F**ile, **S**ave, type a name, and then choose OK. WordPerfect brings up a dialog box, saying that the file already exists, and asking if you want to replace it. If you aren't intentionally replacing an old file with this new one, choose **N**o; then type a new name for your new file. Otherwise, you could be erasing a file that you'll need someday.

6. **Don't manually number your pages.**

With typewriters, you had to type page numbers on each page. If you try the same thing in WordPerfect, you'll get disastrous results. Any time you edit the document, your manually-typed page numbers will shift around, winding up too far down on the page, or even somehow jumping onto the next page.

Instead of typing page numbers, use the page-numbering feature. Press Ctrl+Home to go to the top of the document; choose **L**ayout, **P**age, **N**umbering; click and hold on the **P**osition pop-up menu button; and then choose Top **R**ight to have page numbers in the top right corner of the page. Choose OK to return to the document screen.

7. **Don't delete files in WordPerfect directories.**

Don't delete files you don't understand. When you look in your WordPerfect directories (they all begin with WP), you notice a lot of files. If you're ever in the mood to clear up some space on your hard drive, you may be tempted to delete some of those files. Well, look elsewhere, my friend. Most of those files are critical to WordPerfect running smoothly.

8. **No secret agents!**

Don't use the Password Protect feature. I didn't cover the Password Protect feature in this book on purpose because it's too tempting. The thought of having your own secret, private files that nobody but you can read is just too mysterious to resist. You'll probably eventually find the Password feature on your own and want to try it out. Well, chances are that somebody who's *really* serious about reading your files could get right past your password. Besides, the chances of forgetting your password (so you can't retrieve your own file) are much greater than the chances of somebody else wanting to read your diary.

9. **Don't play around in your important stuff.**

Don't experiment with new features while you're working on actual real-world work. If something gets messed up, you don't want to have to try to root through your document looking for whatever bizarre codes this strange feature-creature might have inserted. Instead, the first time you try something new, try it on either a blank document or an unimportant one. Don't use the feature in a real document until you've got a handle on how it works.

10. Don't forget to save.

Don't type a document without frequently saving it. When your typing is really on a roll, it's easy to forget to update your document from time to time. That's a big mistake. You wouldn't like it if all those brilliant paragraphs were to suddenly go to the great computer graveyard in the sky. But it could happen unless you save your documents early, and save them often. Read Chapter 1, "Things You **Must** Know to Use WordPerfect," to learn how to save and update your document.

11. Don't just switch off your computer.

Don't turn off your computer without exiting WordPerfect first. When the whistle blows, you want to turn off the computer and get out of the office as fast as you can. It's almost enough to make you shut things down before you exit WordPerfect. Don't do it.

When you exit WordPerfect, it does some important file housecleaning. If you turn off your computer before you exit WordPerfect, the next time you try to use it, WordPerfect will ask you all kinds of strange and time-consuming questions before you can get to work.

12. Can't touch this.

As you get better at WordPerfect, you might feel the urge to explore this strange new program. That's fine. There are, however, a few features that you just aren't very likely to ever need, and I recommend staying away from them. When you see these options in menus and dialog boxes, just ignore them: Hypertext, Equations, Sound Clips, Gradient Fills, Fill Styles, Table of Authorities (unless you're a lawyer, in which case you won't pay attention to anything I say anyway), and Spreadsheets. There are more, but most of them are safely tucked away where you won't likely ever see them.

12 Heart-Stopping WordPerfect Messages and What to Do about Them

1. Timed Backup File Exists

This dialog box appears every once in a while when you start WordPerfect. The best thing to do is choose **O**pen. A document appears in WordPerfect—probably one you recognize and should save.

Why does this message come up? The last time you used Word-Perfect, you didn't exit normally. Either the computer hung up, the power went out, or you just turned off the machine before exiting WordPerfect. So, the next time you start WordPerfect, WordPerfect wants to know if anything is amiss. The file you opened was the file you were working on last when you shut off the computer.

2. WPWin Error: This file does not exist—*your file*

This message appears when you try to open a document by typing a file name in the Open File dialog box and choosing OK. The message means that you made a mistake when typing the file name. When you get this message, choose OK to return to the Open Document dialog box. Look carefully at the file name you typed. If you see the mistake, correct it, and then choose OK. If you get the message again, select the file from the list of files and choose OK.

3. *Your text* not found

You're searching for text, but WordPerfect didn't find it in the part of the document it searched. Choose OK and look closely at the text you're searching for (maybe you typed incorrectly); then try again. If WordPerfect still can't find the text, maybe your insertion

point is too far down in the document; you can try searching in the other direction by choosing Find **Prev** (if you were using **F**ind Next before) or **F**ind Next (if you used Find **Prev** before).

4. **WPWin Error: No conversion DLL available for the requested file type**

This message just means that you've tried to open a file that WordPerfect can't read. For example, you'll get this message if you try to retrieve a program. Choose OK to make this message disappear.

Don't bother trying to retrieve the file again; you won't have any better luck the second time. Try opening a different file instead.

5. **Drive B: (or A:) is not ready (drive door may be open)**

This message happens when you're in the Open File or Save As dialog box and you try to change to a drive that doesn't have a disk in it. Put a disk in the drive you're changing to; then choose **R**etry. If you made a mistake and don't really want to use that drive after all, choose **C**ancel.

6. **The Printer is offline or not selected**

You've probably forgot to turn the printer on before you tried to print the document. (Or the On Line light might not be on, in which case you just need to press the On Line button.) Get the printer so that it's ready to print, and then choose Retry.

7. **WPWin Error: The path is invalid in *your file***

When trying to name a document, you typed the whole path for where it goes. The trouble is, you typed part of the path wrong. For example, you might have typed

C:\WPWIN6\WPDOCS\WOOPDEDO instead of
C:\WPWIN60\WPDOCS\WOOPDEDO—it's just one charac-
ter different and hard to notice, but WordPerfect is very picky.
Choose OK; then look carefully at the path you're trying to save in,
fix the mistake, and save again.

8. File (*your file*) is read-only and cannot be overwritten

This nasty-sounding message reads like you've just tried to break
into NASA's main computer. Nothing so glamorous here. Instead,
this message means that you tried to save a document with a name
that already exists and has been protected against being overwritten. Choose OK, and then save the document using a different
name.

9. Warning! Directory contains files. Remove directory anyway?

You're getting just a touch too zealous in your hard disk housecleaning and have tried using the Open File dialog box's Remove
Directory option on a directory that still has files. If you really want
to delete the directory and everything in it, choose **Yes**. If you
decide to take the safe and sane route, choose **No**; then choose
Cancel to go back to the Open file dialog box.

10. WPWin Error: Access Denied

The disk you're trying to save a file on has been fixed so that you
can only retrieve information from it, not put new files on it. The
best solution is to take the floppy disk out of the drive and use a
different floppy disk. Whoever doesn't want you putting files on
that disk probably has a pretty good reason.

If you must put a file on that floppy disk, first take it out of the drive. If it's a 5.25-inch disk, there's probably a piece of tape covering up a notch on the right edge of the disk (that is, the right side when you're reading the disk label). Remove that piece of tape, insert the disk into the floppy drive, choose OK to make the message disappear, and then try saving to the floppy disk again.

If you were trying to save to a 3.5-inch disk, remove the disk from the drive, turn it over, and slide the little plastic square (in the upper left corner of the disk) so that you can't see a hole through that corner. Put the disk back into the floppy disk drive, press a key to make the `Write protect error` message disappear, and then try saving to the floppy disk again.

11. The document may need to be regenerated. Print Anyway?

You're innocently trying to print your document when, for some reason, this message pops up. It means you've got some fancy indexing or table of contents codes in your document, and WordPerfect wants to know whether you want to print anyway. Choose **Yes** to print the document.

If you're curious about using WordPerfect's powerful-but-convoluted indexing and listing and table-of-contents-ing features, check out *Using WordPerfect 6 for Windows*, Special Edition, which, as luck would have it, is also by Que.

12. The Printer is out of paper or is not connected to your printer

Just about every time I've gotten this message, my printer really was out of paper. Refill your printer, and then choose Retry. If your printer has plenty of paper when you get this message, it's time to holler for a computer expert to find out why your computer and printer are no longer on speaking terms.

12 Features You Should Leave Alone unless You Have Time to Kill

1. Advanced Advance.

You can make your insertion point magically move to any point on the page by using the Advance command. This is nice if you need to put a word exactly 2.75 inches from the top of the page or 1.89 inches from the left side of the page. If you need WordPerfect to print on preprinted forms, you may need to deal with Advance.

Choose **L**ayout, **T**ypesetting, **A**dvance to bring up the Advance dialog box.

Choose the **F**rom Left Edge of Page radio button to tell WordPerfect how far from the left side of the page you want the text to be, and then type how far you want the insertion point to be from the left edge. Next, choose the From **T**op of Page radio button to specify how far from the top of the page (not margin) you want your text to be; type the measurement. Choose OK to return to the document screen.

By the way, you don't *have* to set both a Horizontal Position and a Vertical Position. You can set one and leave the other alone. For example, you might be happy with the horizontal position of the insertion point, but want to move it down to three inches from the top of the page. In that case, you would skip setting the **F**rom Left Edge of Page setting and just do the From **T**op of Page measurement instead.

2. Where's the end of the paragraph?

When you're using WordPerfect, it's sometimes handy to know where you've pressed Enter. If you want symbols to appear

on-screen showing spaces, tabs, the end of paragraphs, and other codes, choose View, Show [Para]. Many of your codes will now show up on the WordPerfect screen. (Don't worry; these symbols won't print.)

If you decide you don't like having these symbols after all, choose View, Show [Para] again to return to the normal look.

3. **Make your letters nice and snug.**

Warning! This tip is only for the incredibly compulsive. If you don't notice or care about the amount of space between two letters, move on.

The *kerning* feature lets you reduce the amount of space between two letters in a word. For example, if you look closely, there seems to be extra space between the *W* and *a* in *Warhol*, especially when you're typing a big heading.

Before kerning

After kerning

The space between these characters has been made smaller

To reduce the space between two characters, move the insertion point so that it's between the characters; then choose Layout, **T**ypesetting, **M**anual Kerning. The Manual Kerning dialog box pops up. The dialog box shouldn't be on top of the letters you want

to bring together. If it is, click the dialog box's title bar and drag the box to a different place. Now click the down-arrow button by the **A**mount box. You'll notice the letters move a little closer together. Click the down arrow again and again until the letters are as close as you like; if they become too close, click the up-arrow button.

If you want to kern other letters, you don't have to close the Manual Kerning dialog box. Just click the insertion point between the next two letters you want to bring together, click back in the Manual Kerning dialog box, and begin kerning again. When you're done, choose OK.

4. **Mark your place.**

If you need to refer to certain parts of a document over and over, it can become a real nuisance to find the part you were looking for, and then go back to where you were writing. Instead, use WordPerfect's Bookmark feature to keep track of the places in your document you refer to often.

To put a bookmark at a certain point in your document, move the insertion point to that place. Choose Insert, **B**ookmark to bring up the Bookmark dialog box; then choose **C**reate. In the Create Bookmark dialog box, you name your bookmark so that it will be easy to remember which bookmark you want to return to later. (You can have lots of bookmarks in a document.) The first few words after the insertion point are selected in the **B**ookmark Name text box. You can either leave those words there for the name or type something more descriptive. Choose OK.

To go back to the bookmark you chose, choose Insert, **B**ookmark to bring up the Bookmark dialog box; then double-click the name of the bookmark you want to go to. Your insertion point magically zooms back to where you were when you created the bookmark.

5. **Outlines made easy.**

Outlines are nice when you've got to make an agenda for a meeting or an outline for a book or report. WordPerfect's Outline feature puts an adjustable outline level on-screen whenever you press Enter.

To turn on Outline, choose **T**ools, **O**utline. The Outline feature bar appears at the top of the screen, with Paragraph in the pop-down menu close to the right side of the screen. Click Paragraph to make the menu appear, and then choose Outline from the list. Click the insertion point to the right of the **I.** that appears on-screen. Type the text for that level. Press Enter to go to the next outline item.

If you want to move over an outline level, press Tab. If you want to move back a level, press Shift+Tab. Each time you press Enter, WordPerfect goes to the previous outline level. The numbers in the margin tell you what level of the outline you're at.

If you want to type some text *not* in Outline mode, or if you just want to turn off outlining, press Enter to go to the line you want normal (not outline) text; then click the Text button.

6. **Have it your way.**

If you use certain margins or line settings all the time in WordPerfect, you can set them to be the defaults. Choose **F**ile, **T**emplate to bring up the Templates dialog box. Check to make sure that Standard is selected. (It should be, but you can never be too careful in a sneaky program like this.) Click the **O**ptions pop-up button to make a menu appear, and then choose **E**dit Template.

WordPerfect now displays an empty window with the Template Feature Bar showing. Go ahead and set the margins, justification,

line spacing, and whatever other formatting you want in each document as you normally would. When you're finished, click the Exit Template button in the Feature Bar. A dialog box appears, asking whether you want to save the changes you've made. Make a sarcastic remark, like "No, I was doing this for my health," and then choose **Yes**. The settings you just made will apply to all the documents you create from now on.

7. **Work with watermarks.**

You know how when you hold bond paper up to the light, you can see the name of the company that made the paper? That company logo is called a *watermark*, and WordPerfect has a feature that lets you create something of the same effect. Namely, you can put a graphic image in the background of your page so that it appears lightly behind your text. When is this useful? Hardly ever, but it's kind of fun to experiment with.

To make a watermark, move the insertion point to the page where you want the watermark to begin. (The watermark will then appear on every page of the document following this point.) Choose **Lay-out**, **Watermark** to bring up the Watermark dialog box; then choose **Create**. The watermark window appears, looking pretty normal, except that the top of the screen displays a Watermark Feature Bar. Click the **Figure** button to bring up the Insert Image dialog box. Scroll through the list of graphics until you find one you want; then double-click that graphic. Your computer grinds away for a while, and then displays the graphic—only lighter than usual. Now close the Watermark window by clicking the Feature Bar's **Close** button. You can now write normally, all over the top of the graphic, which will print in the background of your text.

TIP

> Having the watermark on-screen can slow your work considerably. Once you've put a watermark in your document, you'll find your computer goes faster if you work in Draft mode (choose **V**iew, **D**raft).

8. **Talk to yourself.**

If you want to make a remark to yourself in a document, but don't want that remark to print, try out the Comments feature. Move the insertion point to where you want the comment to appear. Then choose Insert, Comment, Create. The Comment window appears (along with the Comment Feature Bar), where you can type away. Choose **C**lose in the Feature bar when you're done.

An icon appears in the left margin of the line where you created the comment. When you want to look at the comment, click this icon. Click the comment box to make the comment shrink back to an icon.

9. **Dates your way!**

WordPerfect's automatic date feature usually puts the date in like this: October 19, 1993. If you would prefer something different (such as 10/19/93), you can customize the date. Choose Insert, **D**ate, Date **F**ormat to bring up the Document Date/Time Format dialog box. Double-click any of the formats in the list box. You can then insert the date by choosing Insert, **D**ate, **T**ext.

10. **Auto-matic Hyphen-ation.**

WordPerfect ordinarily keeps entire words together on a line, but you can have it hyphenate automatically as you write. This is most useful if your documents are full-justified. Move the insertion point

to where you want WP to begin hyphenating words. Then choose Layout, Line, Hyphenation. Choose the Hyphenation **On** check box; then choose OK to return to the document screen.

11. **More Power Bar.**

The Power Bar is easily the most useful thing on the WordPerfect screen. But there are probably buttons you never use, and you may even wish you had some different buttons available. Well, if you're willing to go through a little hassle, you can customize the Power Bar.

Move the mouse pointer so that it's on the Power Bar, but not over any of the buttons—it should be over one of those tiny spaces between buttons. Double-click here and the Power Bar Preferences dialog box appears. To remove buttons, just click and drag them off the bar. To add buttons, scroll through the Power Bar Preferences list box and check the buttons you want. As a rule of thumb, you'll probably need to remove one button for every one you add, or you'll have more buttons than fit on the screen. (If you have a larger monitor, though, you might be able add more buttons.) Choose OK when you're done.

"I HATE THIS!"

Now the Power Bar's a mess!
If you try to customize the Power Bar and it turns out nasty, you can go back to the good ole original Power Bar. Double- click one of the spaces in the Power Bar to go to the Power Bar Preferences dialog box; then choose Default to go back to the way the Power Bar started.

12. For academics only: footnotes and endnotes.

If you don't know what footnotes and endnotes are, you probably never need them. Basically, footnotes are notes that appear at the bottom of each page; endnotes are notes that appear the end of the document. To create a footnote or endnote, move the insertion point to where you want to refer to the note; then choose Insert, **F**ootnote or **E**ndnote (whichever you want), **C**reate. Type what you want for your note, and then choose the Feature Bar's **C**lose button. A little superscripted number appears where you made the reference, and your note is at the bottom of the page (or at the end of the document, if you're creating endnotes).

12 Common Problems

1. **Some menus disappear!**

By now you've figured out that when you click some buttons, menus pop up. The problem is, sometimes those menus just disappear as soon as you let go of the mouse button—while others stay on-screen until you choose an option. If you click a button and a menu appears, then promptly disappears, click the button again. This time, however, hold down the mouse button. Still holding down the mouse button, move the mouse pointer so that the option you want is highlighted; *then* let go.

2. **I can't open a graphic.**

It's tempting to choose **File**, **Open**, and then double-click the graphic you want to use. There's just one problem: you can't. You can only use the Open File dialog box to open documents—not graphics. If you want to bring a graphic into a document, you need to choose **Graphics**, **Figure** to go to the Insert Image dialog box (which looks a lot like the Open File dialog box, but is different, somehow).

3. **Oops! I forgot to turn on my printer.**

No matter how long you've worked with computers, you'll still occasionally do this one. You send a job to be printed, but haven't bothered to turn on the printer. Windows returns with a nasty message that it can't print. If you turn on the printer now and choose **Retry**, your backlogged print jobs should start rolling out in just a couple minutes.

4. I can't turn on Reveal Codes...or the Ruler...or Zoom...

If you find that you can't use any of these features, you must be working in Two Page mode. If you want to use any of these tools, you need to go to Draft or Page mode. Choose View, and then choose either **D**raft or **P**age.

5. I thought I *already* named that document.

You're being a conscientious WordPerfect person today, so just a few minutes after starting your document, you named it. Now it's time to update it to save your changes, but WordPerfect brought up the Save As dialog box, as if you needed to name the document again. What gives? Well, you probably chose File, Save **A**s, instead of **F**ile, **S**ave. They're right on top of each other and look a lot alike, so it's easy to confuse the two. If you get the Save As dialog box when you just want to update an already-named document, choose Cancel; then choose **F**ile, **S**ave (or press Ctrl+S, or click the Power Bar's Save button). That should do the trick.

6. Where am I?

With just a slight miscalculation of the mouse, it's easy to choose the wrong option in a menu or dialog box, putting you in some strange, foreign-looking dialog box, full of ominous messages and sinister voices. How can you get out without bunging up your mission-critical document? Press Esc, or choose Cancel if the dialog box has a Cancel button. *Don't* choose any of the OK keys—that's the equivalent of giving WordPerfect the go-ahead to do whatever it wants with your document.

7. **Non-System disk? What?**

You're starting a new day of work. You turn on your computer, only to get this message:

```
Non-System disk or disk error
Replace and strike any key when ready
```

The cause of this problem is easy: you have a floppy disk in your A drive. Remove the floppy disk, press the space bar, and get back to work.

8. **mY tEXT lOOKS wEIRD.**

If you're transcribing from something printed, you may not notice accidentally pressing your Caps Lock key when you meant to hit Shift. Now all the characters that you want uppercase are lowercase, and vice versa. You don't have to retype the mess, however. Just move the cursor to the first character where things started being backward. Select the text you want to fix, choose **Edit** Convert Case, **Lowercase**. This makes everything lowercase except the beginning of sentences. You might need to go and fix proper names, but that's easier than retyping the whole thing.

9. **Backspace vs. Delete.**

Pressing Backspace erases the character to the *left* of your insertion point. Pressing Delete erases the character to the *right* of the insertion point. It's that simple, but it's hard to remember. If you've erased in the wrong direction, choose **Edit**, **Un**delete, **Restore** right away to restore the lost text.

10. **Did I say Tab? I meant Indent.**

If you need a paragraph further to the right than the surrounding text, it's tempting to press Tab at the beginning of each line.

Don't. When you edit the paragraph, the tabs will no longer always be at the beginning of each line, and the paragraph becomes a shambles. Instead, right at the beginning of the paragraph, press F7. The entire paragraph is now indented over one tab stop.

11. **I inserted my *own* hyphen.**

If you're at the end of a line and are about to type a long word (such as *terpsichorean*), you might want to break it up with a hyphen. That way the whole word doesn't wrap to the next line, leaving the previous line looking short. Most people hyphenate the word by moving to the point they want to break the word, pressing the hyphen key (-), and then pressing the space bar.

If you edit the paragraph so that the whole word fits on a single line, you now have something that looks like *terpsichorean*. Instead, when you want to hyphenate a word, move to where you want the word to break, and then press Ctrl+Shift+hyphen to insert the hyphen. If you later edit the paragraph so that the whole word fits on a line, the hyphen automatically disappears.

12. **Numbers mysteriously appear in my document.**

Whenever you first start WordPerfect, the Num Lock key is on automatically. If you're used to using the numeric keypad for cursor movement, you can run into a problem. If you want to go to the end of the line and press what you think is End, you've actually just typed **1** because the keys are acting as numbers.

You have a couple options. First, get into the habit of pressing the Num Lock key as soon as you start WordPerfect; this turns off numbers. Second, if your keyboard has a separate keypad for cursor movement, get into the habit of using those keys instead of the ones that double as a numeric keypad.

12 Best WordPerfect Shortcuts

1. Save painlessly.

Press Ctrl+S to save. The first time you save your document, this keystroke combo has you name the document normally. After that, pressing Ctrl+S just updates your document in a flash, without bothering you with any pesky questions.

2. Painless lists.

Bulleted lists and numbered lists are two of the mainstays of word processing. Bulleted lists are just lists with little black circles at the beginning of each item. They look good, but they've traditionally been hands-off for normal people because nobody knows how to make those little black circles. And numbered lists are a pain because you always remember some item that needs to go between 3 and 4, meaning you have to renumber the list.

Well, it doesn't have to be difficult. Just type your list *without* the bullets or numbers, pressing Enter after each item in the list. When you're done, select the whole list, and then choose **Insert, Bullets & Numbers**. The Bullets & Numbers dialog box comes up. Scroll through the list, looking for how you want your list to appear—I like the "Small Circle" and "Numbers" options best. Double-click the type of list you want, wait a second, and behold—your list is bulleted or numbered.

If you find you need to add another item somewhere inside the list, move to the end of the line that should be above your new item, and then press Enter—this gives you a new line. Now press Ctrl+Shift+B to insert a new number or bullet and type the new item (you can do this for as many new items as you want). If you're using a numbered list, WordPerfect automatically renumbers as you go.

3. I don't like this document at *all*.

You probably won't want to keep *everything* you write in WordPerfect. Sometimes you'll just be experimenting, sometimes you'll write something so completely awful you just *have* to get rid of it—before somebody else sees it. When you want to clear your document window without saving, just press Ctrl+Shift+F4. WordPerfect doesn't ask any questions; it just gets rid of the document you were working on.

4. Fast footers and high-speed headers.

If you're working in Page or Two Page mode (choose **V**iew, **P**age or **V**iew, **T**wo Page), you can create and edit headers and footers very quickly. To create a header or footer, move your mouse pointer so that it's somewhere in the top or bottom margin area of the page. Click the right mouse button and a menu appears, with Header/ Footer being the first option. Choose this option to bring up the Headers/Footers dialog box, and then choose Header **A** or Footer **A** to begin. Choose **C**reate. Type your header or footer, and then choose **C**lose on the Header/Footer Feature Bar.

If you want to edit an existing header or footer, just click in the header or footer and start editing—you don't have to mess with menus at all. When you're done, click back in the regular part of the document (below the header or above the footer).

5. A quick way to go to. . . Go To.

The Go To dialog box is handy for when you need to jump to a certain page fast. Most people don't know, though, that you can use a mouse shortcut to get to that Go To dialog box (which is nice when you've already got your hand on the mouse). Move the mouse pointer to the `Pg 1 Ln 1" Pos 1"` part of the status bar

and double-click. You can then use the up- and down-arrow buttons by the Page Number box to set which page you want; choose OK.

6. **Clean up that screen.**

Once in a while, WordPerfect or Windows will leave a goober on your screen—it will look like text is selected, when you know good and well that it isn't. Or text will look like it's in one place, when it shouldn't be. You can tell WordPerfect to snap out of its trance by pressing Ctrl+F3—this makes WordPerfect update the whole screen, so things should look right again.

7. **I can't believe I printed the whole thing.**

Usually when you want to print, you want to print the whole document—not just a page or certain pages. You can skip all the rigamorole of the Print dialog box and print the whole thing by just pressing Ctrl+P.

8. **Back to work!**

Often, the last document you work on in WordPerfect on one day will be the *first* document you work on the next day. Here are the quick steps you can follow to open the document you worked on most recently: Choose **File**, and then look at the bottom of the menu. The four files you've used most recently are listed here—the top is your most-recent document, the second is your second-most-recent, and so on. Just click on the one you want.

9. **I'll be back.**

The QuickMark feature is good for moving around in your document, while still being able to return to a certain part quickly. To use QuickMark, move the insertion point to the place you'll want

to return to, and then press Ctrl+Shift+Q. WordPerfect places a QuickMark, which is like a bookmark, into your document. You can then move around in the document as much as you please. To return to the QuickMark, press Ctrl+Q.

You only have one QuickMark per document, so when you press Ctrl+Shift+Q, the current position of the insertion point becomes the QuickMark. Any places you had pressed Ctrl+Shift+Q earlier don't count anymore.

10. **Reveal Codes tricks.**

It's theoretically possible that you'll learn to love WordPerfect. I know, it sounds crazy now, but stranger things have happened. If you really get to use WordPerfect a lot, you'll also probably start working a lot in Reveal Codes, and you'll want a quick way to turn it on—and off. You've got a couple options open to you. If you've got your hands on the keyboard, press Alt+F3. This keystroke combo works for turning Reveal Codes on *and* off.

You can turn on Reveal Codes quickly by using the mouse. At the very top and very bottom of the vertical scroll bar (above the up-arrow button and below the Page Up/Page Down buttons) are small, black bars—you'd never see them if you weren't looking for them. Move the mouse pointer over either of these bars; when it's in the right place, the pointer turns to an up-and-down arrow. Drag the mouse pointer toward the middle of the screen; as you do, a horizontal bar follows the mouse pointer. When you let go of the mouse button, the Reveal Codes screen appears under that bar.

You can change the amount of Reveal Codes on-screen by clicking this bar, and then dragging up or down. You can get rid of Reveal Codes by clicking this bar and dragging it to the very top or bottom of the window.

11. **Repeat, repeat, repeat, repeat...**

You may want to include the same text over and over in a document—like if you wanted to print your address on a whole page of
labels. WordPerfect's Repeat feature lets you do something over
and over.

Before you use Repeat, type the text you'll want to repeat. If you
want a page break (Ctrl+Enter) or a line (Enter) between each
instance of the text, make sure that you insert these elements, too.
Next, select the text you want repeated, including the line or page
break, and choose **Edit, Cut.** Now choose **Edit, Repeat** to bring up
the Repeat dialog box. Type the number of times you want the text
in the document, and then choose OK. Finally, choose **Edit, Paste.**
The text is plopped in the document, as many times as you asked.
Don't you wish *you* could type that fast?

12. **Next page, previous page.**

When you want to go to the beginning of the next page, don't
press the Page Down key—that just takes you up a *screenful* of text.
Instead, press Alt+Page Down. In the same way, when you want to
go to the beginning of the previous page, press Alt+Page Up.

If you've got your hands on the mouse, you can move up or down a
page at a time by clicking the Page Up/Page Down buttons, just
below the down-arrow button on the vertical scroll bar.

Index

I HATE WORDPERFECT FOR WINDOWS!